AN UNCOMMON LIFE

A Memoir in 50 (Short) Scenes

For Miles & Toni —

6/30/21

Bob Lamm

An Uncommon Life

For further information contact:
    Bob Lamm at blamm86@nyc.rr.com

Contents

AUTHOR'S NOTE

Any full name in this book, first and last, is that individual's real name. If you see only a first name, that name has been changed. In a few cases, identifying information about characters has been changed as well to better protect their anonymity. This memoir isn't an expose. It's about my life and, where relevant, how other people were and are memorable in my life.

....

Regarding the cover... in 1962, when I was in 10th grade, my parents bought me a Royal portable typewriter. This was before electric typewriters became popular. I loved my manual typewriter! Loved the feel of hitting the keys. Loved the sound of those keys. Loved the bell that rang when I hit the carriage return to begin a new line. I used my Royal portable until 1998. Was the last of my friends to buy a computer. Finally decided I just had to have e-mail.

In the mid-1990s, when I was a co-author of sociology text-books for McGraw-Hill, their College Division had an office Halloween party. People were supposed to come in costume. Somehow I got the idea to come as my typewriter. I created an illustration of my Royal portable and put it on my chest. There were lots of reactions, often puzzled. Several young editorial assistants asked: "Is that a computer?"

The walls in my home are filled with dozens of lovely paintings and photographs. Some by my mother, some by friends. A few of my published articles are up there. But just one modest piece of art that I created--and it's on the cover of this book.

PREFACE

This book consists of 50 stories from my life, told chrono-logically. I was born in 1947 and I'm still here in 2021. Some of these stories are political; some aren't. Some are (I hope) funny. Some are sad. Some are angry. Some are (I hope) touching. These stories reflect who I was when younger, how I wanted to change, and how I have. Every word of this book is personal and surely that will be true of people's reactions.

In the early 1970s, when I was in my early 20s, personal essays were widely viewed as indulgent and given little respect. But the women's liberation movement challenged that, insisting in consciousness-raising groups that "the personal is political." That it was essential for women to speak about their lives and quite reasonable to draw conclusions from such testimony. I fully agreed and have written personal essays ever since. Some have appeared in the *New York Times, Ms. Magazine,* other periodicals, and various anthologies. (See the list of sources at the end of the book.)

As those personal essays were being published over decades, many friends told me that both in writing and in person I seemed to have *lots* of stories and was a good storyteller. This collection is the result.

I wrote my first important personal essay in 1972. After some painful rejections, it was published in 1974: a long piece with a few detailed vignettes about people I'd known (with names changed). One of those friends was very unhappy with my account of a difficult conversation we'd had while in college. I have a vivid memory of that night, but his was different.

I've taught a class on "Memoirs With a Social Conscience" at New York University. Each time I have to introduce a careful and complex conversation about memoirs. Is a memoir "history"? Is it "the truth?" This book is *my* version of my history, my version of the truth of my life, my accounts of events and feelings from years or decades ago.

As with any memoir, the reader will have to assess my credibility and should understand the limitations of this literary form. For me as a writer, as a reader, as a college literature instructor, personal essays, creative nonfiction, and memoirs are extremely valuable and meaningful.

For this memoir, I've chosen to focus on storytelling rather than after-the-fact analysis. These 50 stories average about 750 words and are simply 50 short scenes from 74 years of my life. As is true for any memoir writer, there are stories I've chosen not to tell.

I hope you'll find these 50 stories of interest. Your reactions are welcome via blamm86@nyc.rr.com

1 Shocking Minnie

Minnie was the only grandmother I ever knew.

My mother's father, Willie Gold, was a warm, wonderful man. A Russian Jew with no money who'd somehow managed to get here through Ellis Island. Both Orthodox and a socialist, an unusual combination. His life in Brooklyn was a continual struggle with poverty, but little kids in his building flocked to him. I loved Willie and especially loved playing checkers with him. He died when I was eight. I never had the conversations with him that I might have.

Willie's wife, Minnie Gold, was a straight-laced, unpleasant woman who only got worse as she aged. I never liked her. Well after Minnie had died, my mother told me how much she'd been hurt throughout her life by my grandmother's judgments and criticism.

My parents both loved to read: newspapers, magazines, novels, biographies, memoirs, history, anything. Our home was always filled with books. As a boy, an only child, I learned to read when I was three. My parents let me take any book I could find on our shelves. No restrictions. I loved to play with my toy soldiers, I loved the new magic of television, but I also loved to just sit and read.

When I was young, perhaps six, Minnie was visiting and we were all in our living room. I was on the floor, quiet, with book in my hands. Suddenly I asked my mother, loud enough so everyone could hear: "Mommie, does Daddy put his penis in your vagina?" I wish I could remember the look on Minnie's face.

This was an early sign that my life would be a bumpy ride.

2 <u>My Parents and the Great Depression</u>

My father, Henry B. Lamm, was born in 1902 in the Bronx. When the stock market crashed in 1929, he was a young attorney living with his mother and sisters and trying to support the family. My mother, Harriet G. Lamm, was born in 1914 in Brooklyn. She skipped two grades in elementary school. At the time of the crash, she was at Bay Ridge High School and would soon begin Brooklyn College at age 16. Like my father, she well understood what the Depression had meant for her family and so many others.

They married in 1943 and I was born in 1947. We lived in the Upper West Side of Manhattan in the same building where I reside today. My father's success in his law practice enabled the three of us to move to the New York suburbs in 1955. To Mount Vernon, in lower Westchester County.

Although my parents had lived through the worst of the Depression, they somehow never soured on the stock market. They invested cautiously and wisely. Their philosophy over decades: buy blue chip stocks with high dividends and never sell. One of their coups was getting IBM at a low price. It rose and rose.

When I was nine years old, my father decided that I should learn about the stock market. I was a pathologically good son. I had no interest in investments, but of course I went along with my father's request. He had decided to buy me a few shares of stock and teach me how to follow my shares in the newspapers' daily stock listings.

He asked what stock I might be interested in owning and my love of bowling immediately came to mind. A bowling boom had begun in the U.S: new bowling alleys and leagues were everywhere. Two companies built those alleys and manufactured bowling balls: AMF and Brunswick. So my father bought me a few shares of each, altogether not worth lots of money.

To please my father, I checked the newspapers every day to see how my stocks were doing. I had chosen well: bowling was more popular by the day. AMF and Brunswick shares soared over the next year or two. I had a big profit! So one day I went to my father and said we should sell the shares. He got upset, which was unusual for him. He said quite loudly: "WE DON'T SPECULATE!!!" These were supposedly *my* shares, but he wouldn't sell them. And at my young age I certainly couldn't.

A year later the bowling boom began to evaporate—and so did the profits on my few shares of AMF and Brunswick. Eventually I realized I'd been right, but I knew I'd better not tell him that. Even decades later, I never mentioned it.

3 The Crooked Judge

My father, an attorney in private practice in Manhattan for 50 years, loved what he called "the law." He was very reverent about anything connected to our legal and judicial system. His heroes included distinguished judges like Louis Brandeis, Benjamin Cardozo, and Learned Hand.

One night my parents and I were having dinner in a restaurant in Manhattan. Perhaps I was ten. My father pointed at a man sitting at a table. He asked "Do you see that man?" I said I did. "That's Mitch Schweitzer." (A name that meant nothing to me.) "He's a judge." (I didn't care; only baseball players mattered.) "He's a crook!"

It was shocking to hear my father call a sitting judge a "crook." Only decades later did he open up a little. In the 1930s, well before he married, my father lived in Washington Heights and wanted to become a judge. To do so he'd have to become active in a local Democratic club. He did and became friends with J. Raymond Jones, the first African American political boss in Harlem. But something happened in that club—my father never provided details—that led him to walk out and never return. Thereby ending forever his hope of wearing judicial robes.

Back to Mitch Schweitzer. In the early 1970s, Mitch became enmeshed in a major scandal. According to a later *New York Times* obituary—and this is how it looked in New York City newspapers at the time of the scandal—Mitch abruptly resigned his judicial post to halt an inquiry into his fitness as a judge. Rather likely that Mitch cut a deal where if he agreed to resign he wouldn't be indicted for improper conduct. Of course once I read this I called my father. He had been proven right!

My father died in 1985. In 1994, Robert Redford's film *Quiz Show* came to theaters. It's a fiction film about the real-life 1950s TV quiz show scandal, where some contestants were given answers in advance by producers. The scandal was a big deal in my family because my parents knew someone who'd been a winner on one of the shows that was rigged.

As the film traces, at a certain point there was lots of suspicion about the quiz shows being corrupt. A grand jury was convened in New York City. It was rumored they they'd found some very incriminating information. But somehow, mysteriously, that grand jury was shut down. All talk of a quiz show scandal died for a few years—till a successful contestant, Herbert Stempel, started blabbing. The end result was a second investigation and public exposure of the dishonesty and corruption of the quiz shows.

As *Quiz Show* continued, it was implied that NBC and/or some sponsors of the shows had paid someone off to kill that grand jury investigation. Then we heard the name of the judge who perhaps was the culprit. It was... Mitch Schweitzer!!!

If only my father could have been there with me to see that film.

4 <u>High School Battles</u>

I went to Mount Vernon High School in the suburbs of New York City. At that time, our city had about 80,000 residents and a classic divide. The New Haven Railroad's tracks ran through the middle of town. Mainly white residents on the north side of the tracks; mainly Black residents on the south side.

As I began 11th grade in fall 1963, a new high school building opened which would serve public school students from throughout Mount Vernon. There were 800 students in each graduating class. Many were Black, many were Italian, many were Jewish. Yet students were "tracked" into academic levels based on alleged academic ability. As part of the highest "track," I was in classes mainly with Jewish students and rarely with an African American student.

Like me, most of my friends were the children of upper-middle class Jewish families. The fathers were mostly professionals, many of them attorneys. The mothers were mostly fulltime homemakers. My friend Carla's mother was a doctor; it was rumored that she had finished first in her medical school class while Jonas Salk (the inventor of the polio vaccine) was second. For at least the first 20 years of my life, I knew of no other female physician.

The boys in my tracked high school classes, many of them friends of mine, were in an intense and endless competition.

We competed for the highest grades. We competed for prestigious positions and honors at the school, in our synagogues, and elsewhere. We competed to date the most desirable girls in our circles. And, in the most crucial battle, we competed for admission to Ivy League and other high-status colleges. These competitions were always there, always hovering, always playing out, always affecting our friendships.

An especially memorable moment came in 12th grade during a session of Advanced Placement American History class. I was hoping to go to Yale; I'd made no secret of that. I had very high grades and was the feature editor and regular columnist for the school newspaper. I felt confident that I would be a winner in the competition to get into that prestigious college and others.

In the middle of class, a messenger entered the room with a note. Our teacher then read aloud a list of names and said we should all see our college counselors as soon as possible. No reason was given. But we subsequently learned that a member of Yale's Alumni Schools Committee would be coming to our school to interview those of us applying. It was thought that this guy's recommendations were quite important: if he backed you, you were in.

My friend Barry's name was on the list. I was puzzled since he'd never mentioned any interest at Yale. His possible application didn't threaten me; I felt confident I'd get in. When I asked him, he insisted it was all a mistake;

he definitely wasn't applying to Yale. Two weeks later the Yale alumnus came to school for our interviews. And that morning there was Barry, like myself and others, wearing a jacket and tie—which we almost never did at school. I immediately knew what that meant: he'd flat-out lied to me. My friend.

I'd like to say that Barry and various others were into that competitive ugliness more than I was. But is that really true?

With graduation approaching, so were decisions about commencement speakers. I had the highest grades of any senior; I was the valedictorian. But to the outrage of my parents, in our school being the valedictorian didn't mean you'd be the commencement speaker. There was a speaking competition; one girl and one boy would be chosen.

My "friend" Jared and I had been in a competitive battle at least since elementary school. By high school, I was the successful writer; he was the successful orator and contest winner. I desperately wanted to be commencement speaker, partly because of my parents' insistence that my grades should have brought me that honor. But, more than anything, I wanted to beat Jared in *his* strong area.

We had to prepare five-minute speeches and deliver them in front of a few teachers. Mine was mainly on Jim Crow segregation and *Brown vs. Board of Education*. I worked very hard on writing my speech, then I practiced. And practiced. And practiced. The competition came and

I won. I beat Jared and was thrilled that I'd beaten him. Revenge for a public slight during a rec league basketball game when we were 11 years old? Yes, that was part of it.

I hate thinking about the person I was in high school. I've tried ever since to be someone different, someone better. Someone not committed to fierce competition with alleged friends.

In 2015, the phone rang and it was Pamela, a classmate from elementary school calling about our upcoming 50th reunion. I don't believe I'd spoken a single word to her in junior high or high school; we moved in different circles. Almost immediately she said "I remember how smart you were!" I cringed. I tried to say, nicely, that I wouldn't be attending, that I don't go to any Mount Vernon High School reunions.

How could I explain that I'd *never* want to be surrounded by people who remember me—who only knew me--as I was then?

****

There's one other part of the story. In fall 1963, when I began 11th grade, some friends and I joined a new youth group at our local Jewish Y. The staff had been taken over by liberal activists associated with the Columbia School of Social Work and Mobilization for Youth (MFY) in New York City. Larry Shulman, the new head of teen activities at the Y, helped us launch the Youth Activities Council (YAC). I became the #2 leader.

In my last two years of high school, YAC did some remarkable, controversial things. We had as guest speakers students who had gone illegally to visit Fidel Castro's Cuba. We had a speaker from the Student Nonviolent Coordinating Committee (SNCC), the most radical of the major civil rights groups of the early and mid 1960s. We invited the liberal rabbi of my Reform synagogue to debate a representative of the Ethical Culture Society on the question: "Is belief in God necessary for morality?"

We didn't engage in serious activism outside the Y. But we took a step out of our protected suburban cocoon and got a taste of the challenges of the 1960s. Alas, like many adults in our town, we were righteous about Jim Crow racism in the South but silent on the racism all around us and in us. We never pondered the meaning of the "tracking" that put so many of us in virtually all-white academic classes in an allegedly integrated high school. Mount Vernon was becoming the scene of one of the worst battles anywhere in the North over de facto school segregation, but only some years later did I realize I shouldn't stand apart from that war.

5 <u>Summer Camp</u>

As a kid, I hated doing anything new. When my parents insisted on sending me to day camp one summer, I was desperate not to go. I went, loved it, wanted to return for a second summer, and did. Then my parents decided I should go to sleepaway camp. Eight weeks! Again, I was desperate to avoid the next new challenge. I cried on the train to Connecticut. But soon enough I loved it and went to that camp for 10 summers, the last two as a counselor.

The camp called itself a "brother-sister" camp and had almost no coed activities. Most campers were Jewish kids from affluent suburban families, but the camp was only nominally religious. The owner had been a college basketball star in the late 1920s, at a time when many of the great basketball players were Jewish.

Sports was everything in the boys' camp. I loved sports and was a rather bad athlete. Couldn't have been a worse combination. But in my first summer, at age 10, I clicked with other boys in my bunk, in part because we all loved to play cards. Especially canasta. During "rest period" (after lunch) and whenever else we could, we'd play canasta. My bunkmates didn't seem to care that I was a bad athlete. Summer after summer I told my parents that I wanted to return to camp and be in the bunk with my canasta buddies.

For the boys camp, the crucial event was Color War. Maroon vs. Gold (the camp's colors). Four days near the end of the summer. Campers and counselors would be divided into two teams. Boys in each age group would compete in a familiar set of contests: baseball (softball), basketball, a track meet, a swim meet, and many more. Points would be awarded in each event and would be awarded or deducted throughout each day for various achievements or rule violations. The atmosphere was intense at every moment. Nothing was sweeter than to win Color War.

As I got older, I gradually began to see the male pathologies of my beloved camp. At age 12, then again at 14 and 15, I had as my counselor the camp's god. Mark was intelligent, handsome, had been a basketball star in college, and was on the way to becoming an attorney. He always had the most beautiful female counselor as his summer girlfriend. Everyone worshipped Mark.

The Seniors (the oldest male campers) lived down a hill by the lake. Every morning we had to go up the hill for flag raising. Mark decided that each time we'd all have to *run* up that hill. Whoever finished last would later be forced to go "under the mill." All the Senior campers and counselors would form a long line and spread their legs. The loser would crawl under that line and get paddled on the ass, *hard*, by everyone. Just for being last in the daily race up the hill. It would hurt and it was deeply humiliating.

I was a slow runner. I knew I was a likely candidate to be paddled. I was determined not to be. I always made sure to be near the starting line, ahead of most of the others. In two summers, I never finished last; I never went "under the mill." And I gradually came to realize that Mark, the god of the boys camp, was championing its unquestioned, callous masculine codes.

My last summer at the camp was in 1966, just after finishing my first year of college. By now, as a counselor, I'd finally faced that a hell of a lot was wrong at our camp, that boys were being hurt there just as I had been. I openly and passionately challenged various camp traditions. I wrote a statement about what was wrong and shared it privately with a few people. I wish I could have done much more, but I was virtually alone.

Color War, predictably, was when male competition turned ugliest. Especially memorable was my final Color War that summer. I was a counselor for the Juniors (boys 10 and 11 years old). Remarkably, near the end of the final afternoon, the Maroon and Gold teams had virtually an identical number of points. The entire Color War would come down to one unfinished event: Junior punchball. Whoever won this game would win Color War. By the late innings, literally everyone from the boys camp was either in the game or watching in the bleachers. The pressure on these young kids was enormous.

Punchball is just like softball except you stand at the plate, hold a rubber ball in your hand, punch it with a closed fist, and start running to first base. We rarely played during the summer, but punchball was a Color War tradition. None of our kids were especially good at it. It was always a seven-inning struggle.

Our team was winning by a few runs. The game came down to the other team's final at-bat. They rallied, scored some runs, had some runners on base. There were two out and we still led by a run. Just one more out and we'd win. The batter punched a ground ball to our shortstop. He threw to first base and our best player caught it… but bobbled the ball. Did he have full possession before the batter touched the base? It was a very close play. The umpire yelled "OUT." We won the game! We won Color War! Our team erupted in joy.

Ernie was a counselor on the other team. I was standing close by as Ernie ran over and yelled at our first baseman: "You bobbled that ball! He was safe! You know he was safe! You have to tell the umpire!!!" Ernie was about 21. The first baseman was 10. He looked mortified. I was incredulous and enraged. I said nothing. The kid remained silent. Ernie yelled some more, then finally walked away. Color War was over. We had won. I felt sick.

10 summers there, beginning at a vulnerable age. These days that camp, long deceased, has a Facebook page. People go on and on about how glorious it was. Again I say nothing. We have to choose our battles. But I wish I'd said something to Ernie.

6 <u>Challenging the Camp Owner</u>

In the summer of 1964, when I was 17, I was hired to work in the camp office, my first job ever. There were three of us. Max, the camp's owner, was in and out all day. He'd hired Gilda, the married mother of a female camper, as his secretary for the summer. And there I was, a good typist who'd never worked in an office. Who'd never worked for *anyone*.

Max could be charming but had a terrible temper. He wouldn't dare throw one of his tirades at me. Our families went to the same synagogue and knew each other. Had I been upset and told my parents, my father would not have been amused. Max wouldn't have enjoyed a verbal one-on-one with Henry Lamm. Moreover, if my parents told others in the synagogue that Max was mistreating their wonderful son, that wouldn't have gone over well.

Gilda, though, was an easy target. She wasn't from our town and knew no one there. She wasn't a strong person, and clearly wasn't accustomed to fighting it out verbally with an unpleasant male boss. In truth, I didn't like Gilda and she wasn't an especially good secretary. At times, Max's complaints were legitimate, but his explosions were far over the top. Just unnecessary bullying.

One day Max blew up and I couldn't be silent anymore. I told him to stop, that he shouldn't yell at Gilda. He was stunned. He made it clear that this was his camp, I was his employee, and he'd do as he damn well pleased.

It's amusing, but also poignant, for me to remember that moment. I was obviously quite naïve. It simply hadn't occurred to me that I wasn't supposed to tell an adult man, the boss of that office, the owner of that camp, not to yell at a female employee. In 1964, I hadn't yet heard of "women's liberation." There was almost no discussion in our culture about men's abusive behavior toward women in the workplace or anywhere else. "Jokes" about violence against women were everywhere and virtually never criticized.

I was quite naïve… but somehow I'd seen something wrong in front of me and wouldn't accept it. This was the first time I'd spoken out against a man's sexism. Max silenced me and I never challenged him again when he yelled at Gilda. How could I have known that my protest that day wouldn't be my last? That it was a window into what was ahead in my adult life.

• •

When I ponder how I became the 17-year-old who challenged the camp owner, how I became an adult who's made many similar challenges, one childhood experience seems crucial.

My father's ancestors were German Jews who came to the United States before the Civil War. He grew up using the Ashkenazi pronunciation of Hebrew common to Eastern European Jews. By the late 1950s, many Reform Jewish congregations with members mainly from Ashkenazi backgrounds were switching to the Sephardic pronunciation used in Israel.

Our rabbi decided to adopt this change, which had to be approved at a congregational meeting. He was extremely popular and almost always had his way. But that didn't matter to my father. In his view, his ancestors were Ashkenazi Jews, they'd always used the Ashkenazi pronunciation of Hebrew, that's what he'd grown up with as a boy, that's what he was comfortable with. He was a strong supporter of Israel, but saw no good reason why he should adopt Sephardic pronunciation just because Israelis had.

My father decided to lead a fight to retain Ashkenazi pronunciation. Lots of people informally told him they were with him. As with his legal careeer, he worked hard preparing his case. At the meeting, he made a statement on the history of Ashkenazi Jews and why preserving that tradition was important. The result was a crushing defeat. His "friends" who'd said they'd support him didn't.

He told me all this; I must have been nine or 10. It was the single moment in my youth when I most admired my father. He had fought for what he believed in. He took on the most powerful person on the scene. He was mainly alone, backed by "allies" who deserted him. He lost. He lost badly. But I knew he was right. It was a painful but inspiring lesson.

7 <u>Asian Americans and Jewish Americans</u>

Gil was the son of a white woman from the Midwest and a Chinese man, both of whom were professors. His father worked at the United Nations. We were high school classmates, not really friends, but were both admitted to Yale and agreed to become roommates.

In high school, Gil had been popular and respected in circles dominated by white Jews and Christians. In fact, he seemed almost a model of successful assimilation of a (middle class) Asian American into the melting pot of the United States. In the classroom, on the ball fields, even in the church choir, Gil was a standout. His older brother had gone to Yale and so did he.

One evening during sophomore year Gil laid out some of his fears as a Chinese American. "Chairman Mao" (Mao Zedong) was in power in what some derisively called "Red China" and there were racist "yellow peril" fears in the U.S. Gil shared his concern that at some future time severe conflict might erupt between the United States and the People's Republic of China. He worried that, under such conditions, he and other Asian Americans would be in serious danger. Obviously, he was well aware, as I was, of the detention camps for Japanese Americans during World War II.

At first, I was shocked that Gil, of all people, should feel so threatened. How could anyone be more respectable? He was a Yale man, a church choir leader, a trustee of the

International Key Club. He was even in Army R.O.T.C. at the time. (He later became a conscientious objector.) I told Gil he was being paranoid. That couldn't happen here. Why, you're as safe as I am. White Americans wouldn't do something like that to our Asian citizens. To our loyal Chinese American community. So I said in 1966.

I didn't respond that way simply because I was naïve. No, I was frightened. Gil didn't feel safe; well, I didn't feel so safe either. I hadn't forgotten that our country, with its long and tenacious history of antisemitism, had kept its "open door" closed rather tight while millions of desperate European Jews were trapped and exterminated by the Nazis. I didn't blame Gil for being mistrustful of the United States. As a Jew, I didn't feel certain that I would be protected.

I couldn't admit that Gil's fears were justified without admitting my own. I wasn't ready for that. I was too busy pretending that I was "one of the guys" at Yale. Moreover, Gil saw me as white (and therefore safe). It was way too much for me to cope with. Since I couldn't acknowledge my own inner turmoil, my only alternative was to tell him that *he* was paranoid. Nothing like helping your fellow man.

• •

This story was drawn from "Christian God and Jewish Man at Yale," a much longer personal essay about being a Jewish student at Yale in the mid-to-late 1960s. In 1974 it was pub-lished in <u>Response</u>, *an excellent Jewish quarterly.*

Although I'd been a high school newspaper editor and columnist, then had occasionally written for college newspapers, I'd never had in mind to become a writer. In 1974, I did a few short TV reviews for the Village Voice. I loved seeing my name and my words in print in a prestigious newspaper. But when a very personal piece of mine was published, raising issues quite vital to me, that was life-changing. Now I was and would be a writer. It was settled.

8 Realizing I Was Boring

One night in 1966, alone in my Yale dorm room, it suddenly hit me out of nowhere: I was boring.

I'd been aware for years that I was sheltered. As a teen, almost all my dealings were with upper-middle class and middle-class Jewish peers. At Yale, I'd been exposed to upper-class white Protestant guys from elite prep school backgrounds. Still a rather limited mixture of people. I'd done almost no travel. But now, way beyond being sheltered, I decided--quite intensely--that I was boring. There were really only two things I knew much about: conventional party politics in the U.S. and sports. I knew so little about anything else.

I was profoundly upset. It was, in the terminology of that time, "an identity crisis." I proceeded to the logical next step: how could I become someone who wasn't boring? The answer--a rather daunting answer--seemed obvious. I needed to begin putting myself in new situations, some of them uncomfortable, with people quite different from myself. I was a bit shy with strangers and often resisted anything new. But this was what I needed. No question.

It took time for me to genuinely begin that effort. But for the spring 1968 semester I left all-male Yale and became one of the first six men at all-female Sarah Lawrence College. In summer 1968, I spent two months in England researching a senior honors thesis on racism in the British police. Then

I spent a month bouncing from Stockholm to Copenhagen to Rome to Geneva to Paris, often on my own. After graduation from Yale in 1969, I became a VISTA volunteer in San Diego. I lived and worked in Logan Heights, the city's only African American and Chicano neighborhood. In fall 1970, I began living on the Upper West Side and got two jobs: as a halftime preschool teacher at a Montessori school and as a youth group leader at a suburban Reform synagogue. And I joined a political collective running a radical coffeehouse. All that in three years, many worlds outside my previous life. As for heading to law school, my goal since childhood, I got in but never went.

I made a commitment to myself to struggle with my fears, to take risks, to enter new situations, to meet many kinds of people I'd never met. Now I'm heading toward my 74th birthday and I've never stopped. And I no longer feel boring. In a crucial way, it all came from that night in the dorm room.

I'm left with a question that fascinates me and that I'll never be able to answer. How did that night happen? How did I somehow step outside myself and decide that I was boring? It's as if there was an authentic person hidden deep inside me, trying to burst out of prison, trying to replace the "good son" living the life his parents wanted for him.

It's been a thrilling but complicated road since I escaped that prison, with many ups and downs, with achievements and disappointments. But it's unquestionably been *my* road. I treasure that.

9 The Professor and the Movie Stars

In my sophomore year at Yale, I took a two-semester introductory philosophy seminar with Charles B. "Danny" Daniels. He'd just arrived at the university and was living in Saybrook, my residential college. Danny was a brilliant, fascinating, exciting, quirky teacher, profoundly different from the often stuffy Yale faculty members. The kind of teacher who might somehow insert an example from baseball or folk music into abstract philosophical discussions. Danny was from the U.S. but had lived for many years in England. He'd been an "ice blocker"—one of the workers who cuts giant blocks of ice into smaller blocks—then somehow switched to studying linguistic philosophy at Oxford.

My roommate Ben and I had many meals with Danny in the Saybrook Dining Hall. He was great fun and *never* talked down to us. On my first visit to London in 1968, Danny invited me to join him and a group of friends for a joyous Indian meal, my first exposure to that glorious cuisine. Danny was always completely professional in class. But, unlike so many faculty members at Yale, he didn't care a bit about rank and genuinely enjoyed spending time with students outside of class.

In 1966, the British film *Georgy Girl* was a big hit. Ben and I saw it together and were completely entranced with the young Charlotte Rampling. One night at dinner the movie came up. Danny said casually, "Oh, I know Charlotte."

We were shocked. We weren't accustomed to being around anyone who knew beautiful film stars and certainly not Yale faculty members who did. We didn't know whether to believe Danny. He'd lived in London for many years. Perhaps Charlotte Rampling was just a friend of a friend whom he'd met at one or two parties.

We basically let that go. Then months later Danny mentioned offhand that Elizabeth Hartman was his girlfriend. She was in her early 20s, at the peak of her career. She'd been nominated for an Oscar for Best Actress for *A Patch of Blue,* working opposite Sidney Poitier, and subsequently had terrific roles in major films like *The Group, You're a Big Boy Now,* and *Beguiled. S*he was Danny's girlfriend??? This time my roommate and I simply didn't buy it. No way.

A month or two later Ben and I were outside the dining hall, waiting for the doors to open for dinner. In came Danny with a small, slight, shy woman, casually dressed. He came right over to us and said, "Bob, Ben, I'd like you to meet Elizabeth." And there she was!

Charlotte Rampling has gone on to a long and distinguished acting career. Alas, Elizabeth Hartman's career took a severe nosedive in her late 20s. She committed suicide in Pittsburgh at age 43. Whenever I see her great work in one of her films, I remember the night we met her and feel profoundly sad. And I think of how lucky I was to know Danny Daniels.

10 The Horrors of Big Law Firms

For the first 20 years of my life, I was certain I was heading to a career as an attorney, just like my father. By the middle of college, I had high grades at Yale and felt I could get into prestigious law schools. My career path was looking good.

In 1967, I got a summer job at the famed Manhattan law firm of Paul, Weiss, Rifkind, Wharton, and Garrison. I'd be an assistant in the accounting department and was ecstatic. This was exactly where I felt I'd want to be after law school: a liberal, Democratic, mainly Jewish firm.

A few weeks into the job, I received a copy of the weekly Paul, Weiss newsletter. The lead article was about the case of *Nader v. General Motors*. Ralph Nader, just beginning to be nationally known, had discovered that the Chevrolet Corvair, one of G.M.'s cars, was seriously unsafe. In response, G.M. had attempted to invade Nader's privacy and intimidate him. The firm's newsletter proudly announced that we were involved in *Nader v. General Motors*. Were we on the side of the dedicated consumer advocate? Hardly. Paul, Weiss was defending G.M., with Ted Sorenson, formerly Jack Kennedy's adviser and speechwriter, as the lead counsel.

In my first semester at Yale, I'd stumbled into a sociology class with one of the only radical professors in the entire university: Bob Cook. He'd given us a powerful set of readings that challenged my liberal beliefs. He spoke critically of "corporate liberalism" and kept asking what kind of social change influential liberals would support when they were making bundles of money from awful corporations.

I was troubled by what Cook was arguing but didn't want to believe him. Now I was at Paul, Weiss, working in the accounting department on the client books. Seeing exactly who these liberal attorneys were representing: overwhelmingly rich people and large corporations. And now G.M. against Ralph Nader. I could no longer deny Bob Cook's powerful critique.

There was more. I worked on the non-legal payroll and could see what my accounting department co-workers were making. One was Faith, a passionate defender of the Vietnam War with whom I repeatedly argued. She'd worked there forever, back when the deceased founders, Mr. Paul and Mr. Weiss, were in charge. But even as the firm was raking in money, Faith was making a pittance despite all her history there.

And then there was a jarring lesson about status. My parents discovered that an attorney at the firm named Sandy, perhaps 30 years old, had gone to my high school, to our synagogue, and then to Yale. It was arranged for him to take me to lunch. I knew no one at the firm, so I was delighted. Lunch with Sandy and a friend of his went quite nicely. I naively thought: "Now I have someone I can go to lunch with occasionally."

A week or two later, when I asked about that, Sandy completely brushed me off. I was baffled… till I finally grasped the class and status implications. He was an attorney; I was a summer assistant in the accounting department. He could take me to lunch once as a favor. But we couldn't possibly be seen as casual *friends*. Even though we'd gone to the same high school, the same synagogue, and the same university! The meaning of this sickened me.

My summer job was for June, July, and August. I quit a month early; my parents were horrified. I hadn't yet given up on my dream of being a lawyer, but I knew I would never, *never*, get near one of those "prestigious" firms again.

11 The Goldfish Bowl

In the spring of 1968, I was one of the first six men at Sarah Lawrence as the college became coeducational. I was there only one semester. (My leaving Yale, even for a term, was distressing for my parents.) Being at Sarah Lawrence was one of the most intense, perplexing, difficult, and profound experiences of my life.

It began like a tornado. On the first day of the term, I stepped out of the administration building and was grabbed by an assistant to the college president, who dragged me to an interview. Reporters were everywhere. That night the male students were on all the local TV stations. Soon afterward one of us learned that his photograph had appeared in a newspaper in Japan.

Academically, Sarah Lawrence was wonderful for me. I took terrific courses on Utopian literature and Russian history. Most important, I worked with sociologist Bert Swanson as he studied the bitter school integration battles in nearby Mount Vernon, my home town, and tried to support those fighting racism. But being one of the famed six men was like living in a goldfish bowl. Sarah Lawrence then had only 550 undergraduates and only 400 living on campus. A female student noted that for Sarah Lawrence women "Your academic life is private but your social life is public." And there we were, rather conspicuous.

My most vivid memories are of my first meals in the dining hall. I'd open the door, see 200 female students at tables, try not to panic, then head for the serving line. Next came the daunting question: where do I sit? Often I couldn't spot any familiar faces. Sometimes I sat alone and female students joined me. Sometimes not. Sometimes I sat with strangers who were friendly. Sometimes they were cold and distant.

I felt extremely vulnerable. Often before or after meals I would retreat to the gym next to the dining hall and shoot baskets all alone. There were choices, choices, choices, and they seemed so personal yet so thoroughly public. I wasn't the only one who felt this. One of the male students tried to keep secret his romance with a female student. I discovered the truth only when I saw her climbing out his ground-floor window of our house rather than using the front door.

For me, the women of Sarah Lawrence were a shock and a revelation. They were bold, independent, outspoken, different. At a dance in the dining hall, a female student I'd just met ended up playing the drums. Similarly, a student working as an office assistant told me she wanted to become a forest ranger. These were rare pursuits for women in the pre-feminist 1960s.

I was sheltered, but Sarah Lawrence women apparently had been everywhere, knew everyone, and had done everything. One night, during a party in our house, I was proudly showing off a small reproduction I'd bought of a painting by Stuart Davis. "Oh, I knew Stuart," said one female student casually. "I met him at a party a few years ago." Another student told me that at 16 she'd had an affair with a man who was 45. She'd told her mother that the man was 27, but her mother was still quite unhappy.

In that explosive spring of 1968, I came to know and value many of the school's political radicals. They challenged my belief in the Democratic Party, my unquestioning view of capitalism, and my failure to look deeply at the racism of the North. I went for the first time to meetings of Students for a Democratic Society (SDS) and I listened. Thanks to one of the leading activists, I first heard the words "women's liberation." These students were intelligent, passionate, committed, and caring. My writing, teaching, and activism over five decades have been influenced by those remarkable young women.

I was in a different world at Sarah Lawrence, a world I really wasn't ready for. I felt off balance for most of the semester. I had to make major emotional adjustments rather quickly. I made some bad decisions. But I met many remarkable young women and I learned a hell of a lot.

12 Yale, Vietnam, and the Draft

In 1967, on the first day I returned to New Haven for our fall semester, I was suddenly overwhelmed by what I'd increasingly repressed for two years. I hated Yale.

I was sickened by all-male Yale College's long history of privilege, elitism, and exclusion, including sexism, racism and anti-Semitism. I was baffled and ultimately repulsed by the cherished prep school traditions that were everywhere. I was appalled by the ugly view of women as a commodity to be exploited. (Women were called "cheese"; a woman was "a piece of cheese.") I saw the inevitable damage from the academic pathology of "publish or perish." I strongly disliked many of the arrogant Yale men that surrounded me in classes and in the Saybrook College dining hall.

One part of my anger began in freshman year. In the fall of 1965, the Vietnam War was just getting going. Our country was mainly unaware of what was happening in that faraway land and the jagged history that had preceded our involvement. But I realized early on that the war was wrong. I wasn't a radical then, just a liberal Democrat and yet a prime target for redbaiting. Many of my Yale peers saw me as a Jew-Commie, essentially as Trotsky--though of course most had no idea who Leon Trotsky was.

As the war "escalated" in 1965, 1966, and 1967, my battles with these men intensified. It was crucial to stop Communism in Asia, they argued. The "domino theory" seemed as popular at Yale as elsewhere in the U.S. If Communists took over Vietnam, presumably the invasion of Golden Gate Park, the Santa Monica Pier, and the glorious beaches of La Jolla would be next. I wondered if many thousands of Chinese and Vietnamese Communists would cross the Pacific in rowboats; neither country had a navy.

While these debates at Yale continued, while more and more young men from the U.S. were drafted to fight in Vietnam, we Yalies knew we were safe. Under the Selective Service policies, anyone could get a draft deferment as long as he was enrolled in higher education. An undergraduate program, graduate school, a professional school, whatever. Once men reached age 26, we went into an entirely different draft category and were almost certain never to be called.

What this meant, as Yalies well understood, was that we who had privilege could simply stay in school until age 26, whether we had genuine interest or not. The defenders of the Vietnam War with whom I argued at Yale knew they'd never have to fight and die in Asia or anywhere else.

My growing alienation from Yale led me to Sarah Lawrence in 1968 for the spring semester of my junior year. While I was there, the Johnson administration—bowing to years of protests—finally revised the nation's inequitable draft policies. Most student deferments were restricted or eliminated. You could no longer take five or six years to get a B.A. while being protected from the draft; now the maximum was four years. Graduate school, law school, business school, medical school—no deferments. Only for divinity school. There would be an annual lottery, you'd get a number based on your date of birth, and that would determine your likelihood of getting drafted. If you got a bad number (mine was borderline), you were screwed.

I returned to Yale in fall 1968 for my senior year, having been away for just one semester. What a sea change! All the guys who'd trashed me for years for being against the war… guess what? Now *they* were against the war! Quite passionately. Not only did they never apologize for their attacks on me; they never acknowledged any previous position regarding Vietnam. Hadn't they *always* been against the war?

The subtext was obvious. When it was poor Black guys from the ghettos and poor white guys from the farms who would die in Vietnam, that war was essential. A holy cause we all had to support. But when it might be *our* necks on the line, then suddenly stopping Communism in Asia wasn't quite as crucial. The hypocrisy of these men left me bitter.

The postscript to the story was predictable. I spent 3½ years as an undergraduate at Yale. I met, at least superficially, hundreds of male students. I know of only one who died in Vietnam: a law student who'd been a freshman counselor in a dorm. Apparently he had enlisted and become a lieutenant.

Very few Yale men I knew ever served in Vietnam. Most of us manipulated the system and found our ways out. With the help and encouragement of a physician, I flunked my physical. My friend Peter went into the National Guard.

Everyone had his story. I've never seen any data about Yale and Vietnam. But John Gregory Dunne, a member of Harvard's class of 1970, wrote of a survey of 600 of his classmates. Only 56 served in the U.S. military and only two in Vietnam. The draft policy had been changed, but most men from elite schools found ways to stay safe.

• •

There's a postscript to my painful undergraduate years at Yale. I've tried to use my endless anger about my alma mater constructively. I've written five published pieces about Yale, none of them flattering. In 1978 and 1980, I had wonderful experiences there teaching pro-feminist seminars on "Men, Masculinity, and Sexism." My impressive students were the most atypical Yale undergraduates imaginable: leaders and activists from the Black Student Alliance, the Council of Third World Women, and the Undergraduate Women's Caucus.

Over more than 50 years, I've tried to support students, faculty, alumni, and staff unions fighting to make Yale a better place. Most notably, in the late 1970s I was a strong supporter of Alexander v. Yale. *In this courageous class action lawsuit, undergraduate feminists became the first students in the U.S. to take their own university into federal court on the issue of sexual harassment. Friends of mine were attorneys and plaintiffs in this pioneering effort. I made three day trips from Manhattan to New Haven to sit in federal court and support them. Their case was partly won and partly lost, but today remains a crucial legal linchpin in all Title IX activism on college campuses regarding rape, sexual assault, and sexual harassment.*

13 <u>Morley Safer and Networking</u>

My parents were determined geniuses at networking long before that term became popular. Whenever anything came up involving my present or future, they contacted lots of people and asked if they knew anyone who might be helpful. It made me uncomfortable, but there always seemed to be a friend of a friend….

During my junior year at Yale, I decided to become an honors major in political science. That meant writing an undergraduate thesis, which was prestigious and would be an important part of my senior year. On the advice of my faculty adviser, I applied for and won a National Science Foundation grant to do summer research in Europe.

My topic was racism in the British police. In April 1968, Enoch Powell, a Tory member of Parliament from Wolverhampton, England, went on the floor of the House of Commons. He delivered an ugly, racist speech about "immigrants" (meaning people of color) and ominously raised the specter of "rivers of blood." Fifty years later, Powell's speech remains infamous in British history.

Just two months after Powell spoke in Parliament, I arrived in London with hope of interviewing police officers, civil rights leaders, civil liberties leaders, and Black Power leaders. Just one crucial problem, which I hadn't yet realized. I'd read a good deal about race relations in Britain and conflicts involving police officers. But I'd never given any thought to exactly how I'd get permission to interview police.

My parents knew someone who knew someone who knew someone who knew the late Morley Safer. This was before his decades on the CBS news series *60 Minutes*. Safer was already a big name for his courageous, challenging, on-the-scene reporting on the Vietnam War. Now he was the head of the CBS bureau in London.

After arrival, I called him, he was very nice, and he said to come by the office. I was staying in a bed-and-breakfast hotel. I had no desk, no typewriter, no phone of any kind, just a tiny room. I met Safer and told him more about my thesis. He said: "You're welcome to use our office. You can come here anytime during normal office hours. No need to make an appointment. Just come, use a typewriter, a phone, a mimeograph machine, whatever isn't in use."

This was a remarkably generous offer, but he went far beyond that. Safer added: "I know this Canadian guy named Griffin. You should meet him." Griffin was an economist who worked in the Police Research and Planning Branch of the Home Office, the agency of national government in charge of all police officers in Britain. I called Griffin, used Safer's name, and he agreed to meet with me. He was welcoming but said what I hoped to do really didn't fit into his jurisdiction. That I needed to talk with his colleague Brian Venner, who handled attitude research for the Police Research and Planning Branch.

Griffin arranged for me to meet Brian, who was quite taken with what I had in mind. He said he'd make some calls. He arranged for me to interview police officers in various precincts in London. Because of his position, he didn't ask. If Brian told police supervisors that he wanted this, it had to happen.

Then Brian decided I should go to Wolverhampton, Enoch Powell's home base, and interview some police officers there. The unmarried male officers all lived in a decaying mansion, essentially a slightly nicer military barracks. Brian arranged for me to spend a week in Wolverhampton, interviewing officers at the precincts, staying at that residence, and talking with those men when they were off work. I played billiards with the officers, watched the 1968 Republican National Convention with them (Richard Nixon was nominated), and conducted interviews at Wolverhampton police stations.

I had only two months in Britain. I could have easily ended up without any interviews with police officers. Only when I realized how things worked in London did I begin to understand how lucky I'd been. Thanks to Morley Safer. And Griffin. And Brian. And my parents' passion for networking to help their son.

14 Racism: U.S. vs. U.K.

The most crucial part of the research for my senior thesis was interviewing police officers in Britain. I did lots of library research. But I felt it essential to interview civil rights leaders, civil liberties leaders, and Black Power leaders.

At this time, especially in the summers of 1967 and 1968, cities in the U.S. were facing serious riots and rebellions in African American neighborhoods. The affluent white Brits I was meeting were completely smug about the racial conflicts in the U.S. "That could never happen here," they said again and again. Even as a 21-year-old first-time visitor I could see that they were wrong. That Black communities like London's Brixton were on the edge of exploding. Soon enough I was proven right.

As in the U.S., multiracial civil rights organizations influential in the early 1960s had by now experienced Black Power takeovers. I'd read a lot of Black Power literature from the U.S. and greatly admired those advocates. But I'd never actually met any and was a bit scared to approach activists in London. Not that I feared they would hurt me. Just that there was intense anger in some of the literature and I was uneasy about how the local Black Power leaders might react to a rather uninformed white boy from the U.S.

I called two of them and each agreed to meet with me. One was the leader of the West Indian Standing Conference, a cultural nationalist group. The other, also West Indian, was the head of CARD (Campaign Against Racial Discrimination), which had previously been the leading multiracial civil rights group in Britain. It had often been compared to the important U.S. civil rights organization CORE (Congress of Racial Equality).

I met with these two men separately. I was nervous. They couldn't have been more more gracious, more patient. They spoke openly and candidly, they responded to my questions, and they asked about my project with interest.

I especially hit it off with the leader of CARD. Toward the end of our chat, we spoke of comparative race relations: the U.S. vs. the U.K. Suddenly he said loudly, laughing through every word: "RACISM? You Americans don't know about RACISM! England is the GRANDDADDY OF RACISM!!!"

15 My First Night in Rome

The grant I'd received allowed me to spend June and July of 1968 in England researching my senior thesis. For August, my parents, who loved travel, had very kindly given me money to bounce around the European continent. My first time on the road and often on my own. I went to Stockholm, Copenhagen, Rome, Florence, Pisa, Geneva, and Paris. Mainly a glorious month.

I arrived in Rome knowing no one there and speaking no Italian. Friends from the U.S. were set to meet me in two days. I found a place to stay and now evening was approaching. My guidebook said that the place to go at night was the Via Veneto.

I was soon wandering aimlessly on a main street filled with bars and clubs. Even at a young age, this type of nightlife didn't really appeal to me. Suddenly a man standing outside a club said hello in well-spoken English. I walked over, he was friendly, and we began a pleasant chat. I quickly realized that he owned the club and was trying to persuade obvious tourists to come in.

I decided "Why not?" I had nothing else to do; I'd sit down and have a beer. Within seconds of seating myself, a young woman appeared and sat next to me, *very* close. She spoke almost no English. I was shocked; I'd never had this happen before. I was inexperienced but not entirely clueless. I wondered: is this a setup for me to have many drinks and spend lots of money? Is this a setup for prostitution? Is this an either/or?

Whatever the plan was, I wasn't into it. Not at all. I flashed on leaving, but I wasn't anxious to make a scene. I thought: "I'll have a beer, I'll buy her a beer, and then I'll leave." Seemed reasonable.

Now a waiter appeared. He asked what I'd have and I ordered a beer. Then, looking at me, he asked: "And for the lady?" It seemed for me to decide; this was the game. So I said he should bring her a beer as well. Now came a surprise. In the most imperious manner possible, he said: "The lady only drinks wine!!!"

OK, I saw where we were heading: to get me to buy a bottle of wine and be given the most expensive bottle they had. Or to be given a mediocre wine but get charged a premium rate anyway.

I decided: she's obviously too good for me. I drink beer; she only drinks wine. Without a word, I stood up and walked out.

16 Ted Gold and Willie Mays

Just after graduating from Yale in 1969, I flew to the Bay Area. I'd never been in California and was thrilled to finally get there. I'd stay for a week with a friend in Berkeley, then head to San Diego to begin a year as a VISTA Volunteer.

While in Berkeley, I read that Ted Gold and Linda Evans of the Weathermen were giving a public talk. I wasn't a radical yet, but was following radical politics closely. I detested the Weathermen's violent rhetoric and pseudo-revolutionary bravado. Still, I'd never heard any of them speak and decided to attend. The event was held in a college auditorium; the room was filled with Berkeley leftists quite hostile to the speakers. It was a stormy meeting.

Ted Gold, I later learned, was from the Upper West Side of Manhattan. His father was a physician, his mother a math instructor at Columbia. Both had been involved in the Left decades earlier. Gold had gone to the outstanding Stuyvesant High School. When he began at Columbia in fall 1964, he quickly became active in raising money for the Student Nonviolent Coordinating Committee (SNCC), one of the most courageous and radical civil rights groups active in the Deep South. Gold subsequently became involved in Students for a Democratic Society (SDS), then the Weathermen, and was a leader of the intense protests and building occupations at Columbia in spring 1968.

Listening to him, I liked Ted Gold a lot. I didn't agree with a word he said, but somehow I liked him anyway. We were both from upper-middle class Jewish families and had gone to elite colleges. I was gradually becoming more radical and he seemed like a far more radical version of me… with dubious and likely disastrous consequences.

Eventually came the moment I'll never forget. Referring to one of the greatest baseball stars in the history of that sport, Ted Gold said "I can never be a good communist as long as Willie Mays is alive." I was aghast. I didn't understand the pathologies of ultraleft politics, but I knew that Gold's statement reflected something terribly wrong. You couldn't care about social justice, your commitment was worthless, if you loved a great athlete? Or a great violinist? Or who else and what else?

That was June 1969. On March 6, 1970, I was living in a New York suburb and working for a professor at Sarah Lawrence. Then I learned of a townhouse explosion on West 11th Street in Manhattan. Members of the Weather Underground had been building a bomb and something went wrong. Two of them made it out alive. Three died; one was Ted Gold. He was getting home when the bomb went off and was crushed by falling debris.

Ted Gold died at age 22. As of 2021, Willie Mays is close to 90 years old. Whenever I hear of the Weathermen, I think of Ted and Willie. I am left hoping that in the last year of his life Ted Gold committed the horrible counterrevolutionary act of sneaking out to a ballpark somewhere to watch Willie Mays.

17 <u>My VISTA Battle</u>

I was a VISTA Volunteer in San Diego in 1969. VISTA was essentially intended to be a domestic version of the Peace Corps that would assist people in low-income neighborhoods in the U.S. I joined in good part to beat the draft at the height of the Vietnam War.

I was living and working in Logan Heights (now known as Barrio Logan), the only African American and Chicano (Mexican American) community in San Diego at that time. City planners had cleverly surrounded the neighborhood with highways on all four sides. This meant that white San Diegans could drive by and literally never see Logan Heights. Most feared and avoided the community.

While in college, I'd been exposed to and deeply affected by the Black Power literature of the late 1960s. Including their challenge to sympathetic white people: if you really want to support our cause, then don't come into our neighborhoods as our saviors. Go into your own communities and fight the racism there.

I had that in mind when I arrived in San Diego. I thought it might be valuable for me to do some political organizing in white and Jewish areas. San Diego was intensely conservative; African Americans and Chicanos were essentially powerless. On crucial issues like police brutality, they desperately needed white support and there was little to none.

I hoped to begin some anti-racist educational work and to build support for political initiatives coming from activists in Logan Heights.

My VISTA bosses were firmly opposed to this approach. For them, VISTA was a seven-day a week, 24-hour-a-day job. In their often repeated view, any time spent outside the poverty area should be spent *inside* the poverty area. The VISTA volunteers, like myself, were overwhelmingly middle-class white boys just out of college who joined in good part to avoid Vietnam. Almost none of us knew a damn thing about African American and Chicano life, but VISTA wanted us to become political organizers for these communities.

At first—out of fear of being fired from the program and therefore eligible for the draft—I kept silent and tried to go along. But eventually, as I saw that most of us were accomplishing little, I began to openly question the VISTA ideology. Many volunteers had never given much thought to these issues and were a bit shaken by the challenges I was raising. My bosses were *not* happy.

Neighborhood House, one of the antipoverty agencies we worked with, had set up a Black/white encounter group that was meeting weekly. Some of us young white VISTA volunteers met with African Americans from the neighborhood who were about our age. They were extremely suspicious, repeatedly demanding to know "What the ____ are you doing in our community?" None of us had good answers. Kim, an impressive young African American VISTA manager from the L.A. office, turned up at one of these meetings. She was completely committed to the VISTA approach and seemed horrified by what she heard. She finally erupted into an oration about how the VISTA volunteers in San Diego had really been accomplishing a lot. (Not true.) But in recent weeks much of the progress had stalled, in her view, because "someone has been leading all of you on a very bad trip." I wasn't named, but everyone from VISTA knew I was that "someone."

Kim's attack was remarkably ironic. It was as if these eloquent, angry young African Americans were getting their ideas from me. Couldn't have been further from the truth. Even when I agreed with them, they didn't care and made that clear.

I had subsequent meetings with the VISTA bosses and we battled it out. Finally, surprisingly, Kim asked to meet with me one-to-one. I couldn't say "no." She proposed having dinner, picked me up in her car, and drove us to a restaurant.

Most of Logan Heights felt quite safe for us white boys. But Kim brought me to a soul food restaurant in the one part of the community that did *not* feel comfortable. When we walked in, I felt I might have been the first pale skinned visitor ever to set foot inside. I was 22 and not all that worldly, but I knew we weren't there just because Kim loved soul food, if in fact she did. She chose that setting to intimidate me, plain and simple.

A tense dinner began. Kim presented her arguments for why it was just fine for VISTA to send white people into Black communities as political organizers. I rebutted her arguments one by one. This was ground we'd been over again and again. Kim was intelligent and eloquent, but I was holding my own. Total stalemate. Alas, Kim was getting angrier because she wasn't winning the argument.

Then came the moment of truth. Nothing else had worked, so Kim insisted: "Listen, this is *my* community and I know what we need!" I couldn't believe she was saying that. I felt on the edge of a cliff. She was already pissed. My mind began racing. What if she doesn't like my response and angrily walks out? I have no car. It's a dicey street for anyone, but especially for a white boy alone at night.

But I wouldn't back down. I just wouldn't.

I said, somehow calmly, "Kim, I really respect you and your feelings for your community. But the plain truth is that in the Black community there are many political ide-ologies." (That summer there had been gun battles in San Diego between the Black Panther Party and members of US, a Black cultural nationalist group.) "There are many different class interests in the community. There are lots of different viewpoints. And, ultimately, I have to listen to those people in the community who make the most sense to me."

Kim was livid. She said little. What could she say? She couldn't pretend that she was speaking for "the community" and she knew it. Indeed, she was well aware that in 1969 many African Americans in Logan Heights and across the U.S. did *not* want white people as their political organizers.

Fortunately, she didn't walk out. She drove me back to where I was living. No doubt Kim and the other VISTA bosses wanted to purge me. In the Orwellian VISTA jargon of that time, to "de-select" me. In the end, they couldn't. The head of the antipoverty agency with which I had been placed, a middle-aged white man from Tennessee, thought I was terrific. So did the lone white staff member from the Urban League, an important civil rights group of the 1960s. They never shared any details, but I'm certain that those two guys saved me.

18 A Friend's Revelation

I graduated from Yale in 1969, just weeks before Stonewall. To my knowledge (then and still today), in the four years I was there no one in the entire university was gay and out. No one. I later learned that there was a gay male underground.

At that time, I was ignorant and clueless about homosexuality and most of my Yale friends were as well. During senior year, a classmate in our residential college began wearing black (many years before it became "in") and began hanging out with a young guy who lived in New Haven. They were often seen together. Most of us surely wondered if they were a couple, but had absolutely no idea how to process that. Even though it was happening right in front of us.

At age 23, in my first year after college, I became briefly involved with a woman I'd met years earlier. Eileen was three years younger, but was *way* ahead of me politically, emotionally, sexually, really in every way imaginable. She was very bold and deeply involved in radical politics. She was where I wanted to be, but I wasn't there yet. And really that's why it didn't work out between us. Nothing unpleasant happened; I simply couldn't cope with being behind.

We remained on good terms. Perhaps six months later, she was living in Berkeley and I was in town. I went to her apartment and she told me she was now a lesbian. This was the first time anyone had come out to me, the first time I'd learned in any clear way that someone I knew was gay. And, in her case, openly gay.

I had huge respect for Eileen. So my immediate and very strong reaction to her news, really my only reaction, was: "If Eileen is a lesbian, then it must be a great thing to be a lesbian."

19 A Painful Failure—Or Was It?

In fall 1970, I began teaching three to five-year-old kids at a Montessori school in Manhattan. Simultaneously, the women's liberation movement was exploding all around me. It seemed as if every female friend from high school or college was now in a women's consciousness-raising group and many were passionate about the emerging feminist activism.

I attended a conference in Boston on early childhood education mainly because I'd read of a workshop on sexism in early childhood education. Held in November 1970, run by two women from New York City, this was surely one of the first such workshops anywhere. It was fascinating and inspiring. I returned to the Montessori school eager to share what I'd learned in that session.

The director, a mother of daughters, was extremely interested. She asked if I'd make a presentation at a lunchtime faculty meeting. The discussion was a complete fiasco. The teachers, 85% women, were profoundly hostile. One spoke about "desexualization," whatever that meant. Even though the ideas that had been presented at the workshop—for example, that it was OK for girls to play with blocks and boys to play with dolls—seem utterly tame decades later. In my youthful idealism and naivete, I couldn't understand why these women were so threatened. I was shocked and disappointed.

That seemed the end of it. But the president of the school's Parent Association—a young, liberal mother--was very excited when I told her of the workshop. Her group had monthly meetings, sometimes with speakers. Could I get those two women to speak at a Parent Association meeting? I didn't know them, hadn't even spoken privately with them at the workshop. But I said I'd try to find the women and ask.

They came and spoke. Just as with the teachers, it was an utter disaster. The audience was mostly female and again was hostile. Most notably, two heterosexual married couples sat together in front. One of the men was a prominent Freudian analyst. They asked unpleasant questions; then, only half an hour into the event, they stood up and walked out together *from the front row!*

Once again, I was shocked and disappointed. It didn't shake my belief that sexism in early childhood education needed to be examined and challenged. But why were all these educated, intelligent people—especially all these educated, intelligent *women*—reacting as they were? My efforts seemed an utter failure.

****

Years later, I read an article in the *Village Voice* about a terrific feminist organization. The article mentioned Martha, whose five-year-old son had been in my Montessori class. Very nice, intelligent woman, but she'd never seemed political. Yet now she was an important feminist activist. Two or three years later, I ran into Martha on the street. I was delighted to see her and vice versa. I told her I was writing about sexual politics and teaching a pro-feminist college class on "Men, Masculinity, and Sexism." She was quite intrigued and said: "You've got to meet our group!"

Their office was in Long Island. One morning I met Martha in our neighborhood and she drove us out there. On the way, I struggled to ask a question I'd been wondering about all along. Gingerly, I said: "I was really interested when I read of your current activism because when we knew each other at the school you hadn't seemed political."

She acknowledged that had been true back then. I asked what led to the change. The first crucial reason she mentioned was having been at the Parent Association meeting where the two feminist speakers discussed sexism in early childhood education. So the two-part fiasco at the Montessori school—the *seeming* fiasco—had at least in one respect been a smashing success. And perhaps others at that faculty discussion or Parent Association meeting were ultimately affected and transformed… even if at first they hated what they were hearing.

I could so easily have never known how that meeting had profoundly affected Martha. What a lesson for writers, for teachers, for political activists. Our "failures" may have actually had profound success that we will never see or hear about.

20 One Night Stand

As a teenager in the 1960s, I loved watching the night-time TV series *Route 66.* Martin Milner played Tod Stiles, a blond, sedate Yale graduate from a wealthy WASP family. George Maharis was dark, brooding Buz Murdock, who had survived a tough childhood in an orphanage in New York's Hell's Kitchen. Together they rode around the country in Tod's Corvette, finding love and adventure at each stop along the way. In a memorable premiere episode in 1960, Buz and Tod were almost lynched in a Southern lumber town—a veiled but bold statement about the lynching of African Americans during Jim Crow.

I was a sheltered kid from the New York suburbs and the romantic images of *Route 66* eventually led me to hit the road. During the summer of 1973, at age 26, I spent nine weeks wandering around the Midwest, the Southwest, and California. I'd decided in advance that I wanted a *Route 66* type journey with lots of new adventures. To achieve that, I'd need to push myself to be much more outgoing than usual, contact friends-of-friends, approach strangers, take risks, and definitely do things I normally wouldn't.

It was an eventful summer. I went on my first camping trip to New Mexico's untouched Gila Wilderness, where Geronimo had hidden out from the cavalry for 20 years. I spent four hours on a Greyhound bus singing folk songs with a young female guitar player from a "peace church" in Nebraska. While in San Diego, I hitched a ride from a feminist lawyer and poet and it led to a romance with a painful end. I ran into Tom Hayden on the beach in Santa Monica, then met with Jane Fonda, and later joined their work against the Vietnam War. I nearly ended up in a San Francisco hospital after a bout with a nasty cat allergy. I met a 34-year-old Texan go-go-dancer who had an acupuncture practice and harbored runaway teenagers.

And I met a cheerleader from Iowa.

• •

I'd been staying in Boulder (a college town about an hour from Denver) for a week with a very kind friend-of-a-friend. It was time to move on; I'd decided that the next morning I'd take a Greyhound bus to Albuquerque. Late that afternoon, I began trying to hitch a ride back to where I was staying. Then I saw, just ahead of me, a second hitchhiker: a beautiful young woman with long, blond hair covered by a silly, floppy hat. Although 22, she looked 16. In my New York Jewish eyes, she absolutely had to be a cheerleader from somewhere in Iowa.

After years of watching *Route 66* on television, I knew this was one of those fateful moments that Tod and Buz were always seeking. I had to approach this Midwestern goddess. Even if it didn't lead to the great romance of my life—and that hardly seemed likely—hitchhiking with her would surely get me a ride much more quickly. I walked over and said hello. She smiled and introduced herself, which surprised me. We established that our route was the same and our destinations close. And of course we got a ride almost immediately.

Her name was Sarah. I quickly checked and, yes, she was from Des Moines, Iowa. (And eventually I learned she'd been a high school cheerleader!) Sarah had graduated from Iowa State with a degree in biology and had a summer job waitressing at a local restaurant. She seemed intrigued by meeting a writer and teacher from New York.

When our driver let us off, we had a short walk before our paths diverged. Suddenly I didn't feel in such a rush to get to New Mexico. I told Sarah I wanted to see her again and asked if I could call her. She hesitated, but gave me her phone number. I went into Denver, stayed there that night, and could have called Sarah. Instead, I somehow decided on a different plan. I'd take an early bus to Boulder and then call her once I arrived.

I was sitting on the 8:00 a.m. bus, my thoughts completely and blissfully filled with Sarah, when, remarkably, I saw her heading down the aisle in my direction. I was so overcome that I couldn't speak. She walked up to me, smiled nervously, took in my silence, and finally asked: "Is it OK if I sit next to you?" I somehow found a way to say "yes." Now we had an hour together. Our conversation felt very relaxed.

We decided to have breakfast, but Sarah needed to stop home first. Soon, ironically, we were back hitchhiking at the very spot where we'd met a day earlier. While I was waiting in her living room, I noticed the latest issue of the feminist periodical *Ms. Magazine* on her coffee table. She was obviously far from any stereotype about cheerleaders from Iowa.

We went back into town and had a pleasant breakfast. Sarah had a long break between waitressing lunch and dinner. I asked if we could spend that time together and she agreed. That afternoon, she took me to a beautiful park overlooking Boulder. We shared our favorite novels and films. We joked about WASPs from Iowa and Jews from New York. As we walked near a stream, she took my hand.

Back in town, we sat at a fountain near the university. I spoke of the culture shock I'd just experienced in St. Louis and Lawrence, Kansas—my first visit to the heart of the Midwest—where I'd felt intensely aware of being Jewish. Sarah listened and her light blue eyes were very serious. I wondered if anyone had ever noticed that.

Soon she'd have to leave for her dinner shift. I told Sarah I wanted to spend the night with her. With a pained look on her face, she confessed that she had a boyfriend. That's why she'd stayed in Denver the night before. She moved away and seemed almost angry, certainly distrustful. But then she came closer, took my hand, and looked at me like she didn't want to leave.

She asked if we could decide later. As a stranger in the area and without a car, I didn't want to head back to Denver at a late hour. I told Sarah that if she was OK with letting me sleep somewhere in her apartment, I was OK with wherever that would or wouldn't be. She agreed, gave me a short, tender kiss, and went off to work. I felt sure that a beautiful night was ahead. Perhaps not the definitive romance of my life, but surely more than the standard 1970s one-night stand. This wasn't going to be *Route 66* where Tod or Buz had a brief fling but never looked back. I wanted to show New York to Sarah.

After her dinner shift, we headed home. Again she was torn about being with me. I was just passing through; she had a boyfriend. Finally we just sat on her porch and held each other for a long while. It turned into a wonderful, tender night. I dissolved each time I saw her glowing smile. It seemed impossible that we'd only met the day before.

In the morning, Sarah looked so beautiful, half-awake, her blond hair tangled all over her shoulders and back, wearing an agonized "I've got to get to work" look. She started kissing my neck and it drove me wild, but there wasn't enough time. We kissed each other gently and laughed. We didn't say much.

We had an early lunch. I said I wanted to stay in Boulder and see her again, but I knew this might be difficult for her. Sarah said she really couldn't handle anything more between us right then. She worried openly that I might take this as a rejection, but I didn't. We spoke of seeing each other again; I invited her to visit me in New York. We walked silently for a few minutes and kissed goodbye twice at the bus station. Then she was gone. I headed into Denver and then to Albuquerque later that day.

My last stop on my long summer adventure was in San Francisco. I pondered a visit to Boulder on the way home and called Sarah. She seemed casual about my call, too casual. Then she suggested that perhaps I could see the mountains with her and her boyfriend. That bizarre suggestion wasn't what I hoped to hear. It was a sad flight back to New York. Over the next few months, I wrote her three letters but received no replies.

Sometimes I think of Sarah when there's a reference to Boulder or to cheerleaders from the Midwest. Or when I'm watching my DVDs of Tod and Buz in their Corvette, out on Route 66 heading for their next adventure.

21 My First Tarot Card Reading

During my *Route 66* summer of 1973, I made my first-ever visit to Santa Fe. It was already becoming a New Age center. I knew little about that subculture and had never had any interest. But in Santa Fe virtually everyone I met was involved in one or many New Age pursuits.

Friends took me to a party where I met a young white woman from Cleveland named Rebecca who told me she was a witch. (Perhaps a Wiccan; she didn't explain.) She was quite nice and by chance knew one of my Yale roommates. She asked if I'd ever had a Tarot Card reading. I hadn't, though I'd seen Tarot decks. I thought: "This is exactly the kind of thing I'm supposed to do this summer. Something I'd never do in my familiar life in Manhattan."

We met a day or two later. Santa Fe has a little river that runs right through the center of that small city. We met on a lawn 10 feet above the river, a lovely spot. We sat on a blanket. Rebecca explained how the reading would work, showed me the various cards, and explained each. She had me shuffle the cards, then dealt them out and began my reading. Everything was going fine; her comments about my cards and my life were intriguing.

Out of nowhere, a huge puff of wind arrived. Wind can affect light, inanimate objects in quite different and unpredictable ways. Some cards didn't move at all. Some simply turned over right where they were. Some were blown off the blanket just a foot away. But one and only one card, the Ace of Pentacles, took a giant leap as if an invisible hand had grabbed it. The Ace flew way into the air, off that lawn, and down into the river below.

Rebecca completely freaked out. There was no path from the lawn to get down to the river. She ran to the edge, trying to follow the card with her eyes. The Ace of Pentacles was heading downstream. I could see it for a few moments, then inevitably it sank into the water and was never visible again.

She was absolutely distraught. She explained how special the Ace of Pentacles was—though I suspected that the loss of any of her cards would have been just as devastating. Then she told me she'd had that deck for many years and cherished it. She'd lost the deck twice and somehow magically it had returned to her intact both times. I highly doubted Rebecca would ever see that Ace of Pentacles again, but of course I didn't say that. She was crushed. That's how my first and only Tarot Card reading ended. I've never had another.

22 Student Power in the Classroom

While I was in college in the late 1960s, the cry of "Student Power" emerged all over the United States. It thrilled me. I felt that students should have a voice in decisions about our education. At that time, with our country intensely divided over segregation and racism as well as the Vietnam War, many of us wanted our collegiate studies to be more relevant to the issues facing our country. Yet most of the highly rated Yale political science faculty couldn't have cared less about our views.

In spring 1973, at age 26, I'd taught a class on "Images of Masculinity in Contemporary America" at the New School in New York City. It was one of the first such college classes anywhere. Then, in 1974, I began teaching at Queens College. Because of my growing interest in feminism, the title of the class was now "Men, Masculinity, and Sexism." I taught it three times at Queens, then at Yale in 1978 and 1980.

My first class at Queens College was in their summer session. Six weeks, Tuesday through Thursday nights, 2½ hours each night. The students were perhaps the most honest I've ever taught. The class was explosive, in part because we had some provocative radical feminist students. There were passionate, heated battles—but the right battles, battles over the issues being debated almost everywhere.

The class was so exciting that students began asking if they could bring guests. This was only the second college class I'd taught. I was young, idealistic, and inexperienced. That's how I found myself facing a highly problematic visitor.

One student, Britta, a liberal feminist, asked if she could invite her boyfriend to join us. As our discussions got going that night, Billy didn't like what he was hearing. He began launching attacks on feminism. He was smug, arrogant, and patronizing. At first, the two most radical women, Risa and Paula, got into it with Billy. Then other women began challenging Billy. Finally, even the male students realized he was destructive and said so.

After an hour or so, literally everyone but Britta was disgusted with Billy and making that quite clear. But he just kept going. He finally got me so angry that I absolutely exploded in a way I'd never done in class before and have never done since. I said: "You've done something here that I would never have thought possible. You've managed to unite everyone against you. I think you're just a condescending… schmuck!!!"

There was a rather dramatic hush. Our class had already included intense analysis of power relations in our culture, including the question of how much power an instructor should have in a classroom. But even the most radical students were stunned that a teacher had called someone a schmuck.

Eventually, getting past my anger, I realized something I should have grasped earlier. I needed to stop this discussion and move us in a different direction. The issues worth our time were getting lost in the battle against Billy. So I told everyone we should avoid any further focus on Billy and return to analyzing the readings.

I was overruled! Too many students wanted to continue blasting away at Billy. They insisted: why should we end this discussion just because *you* want to do so? Why should the instructor have that power? They wouldn't relent; I decided to back off. For about 15 more minutes, they railed at Billy and he kept returning fire. Finally, I once again said that we should ignore Billy and move forward in a different way. This time no one protested. I believe they'd realized that I'd been right the first time.

Over the next 24 hours, I pondered that session and realized something about Billy. He loved every minute of that conflict. He'd have gone on and on, even with everyone in the room but Britta trashing him. The attacks didn't upset him, hurt him, anger him. Why? Because Billy was the complete center of attention. That was all that mattered.

Our social media age is Heaven for men like Billy. (And some women, I guess, but overwhelmingly I see this in men.) Fights with strangers, whether on social media or in person, are a complete thrill. The attention is everything.

• •

It was this class that made me realize I had to be a teacher. The excitement of running passionate discussions about issues that felt crucial—there was nothing like it. Being an instructor in those class sessions was demanding, sometimes draining, but so profoundly enriching and worthwhile. This was my first time teaching for-credit college students. I pushed to have one-to-one meetings with students to discuss the readings, the issues the writers raised, and the students' papers. Many said this was the first time that any faculty member had ever done that. They were stunned by the extensive written comments I made regarding their papers.

Ever since, I've said that I hope my students learn at least half as much from me as I learn from them. That 1974 summer class at Queens College was where that feeling began. When it was over, one essential part of my career path was set.

In 2011, a letter to the editor of mine about teaching was published in the <u>New York Times</u>. The novelist Marie Myung-Ok Lee had written a beautiful op. ed. piece about a high school teacher who had wonderfully transformed her life. In response, I suggested that there is a simple way to document the crucial and permanent impact of teachers. Ask an adult of any age about the very best and very worst teachers they had in their younger days. They will inevitably answer as if they were in class five minutes ago. That's how I feel about the best teachers I had. I hope there are a few students who remember me that way.

23 The Women Students Leave

My second Queens College class on "Men, Masculinity, and Sexism was in the spring 1975 semester, two afternoons per week. It was completely different from the first, though the readings were quite similar.

The male students in my first class mainly displayed a searing honesty. Their reactions to the readings, to my lectures and comments, and to the powerful words of women students were often moving. The male students in my second class couldn't have been more different. They were nice, intelligent men—one a middle-aged African American firefighter who'd returned to college to finish his degree. But they deflected discussions, evaded disagreements, and pretended to be sympathetic. This made honest interactions impossible.

I decided on an approach rarely used in classes at that time. In the second half of some sessions, we'd divide by gender. The female students would all go off somewhere to discuss that session's readings while I would meet with the male students. I tried to find a way of reaching these men but basically failed. Meanwhile, the women began asking for more and more time for their separate sessions and I agreed.

One afternoon, soon after class began, the women announced that for the last six weeks of the semester they would be holding their own separate class. They didn't explicitly ask for my permission, but it felt like they were really asking. I had ultimate power: I could have stopped them. I could have threatened them with flunking grades or other academic penalties. Although I didn't realize this till much later, the male students were waiting for me to forbid the women from having these separate sessions. And in some cases seething when I didn't do that.

I told the women that they'd have to give me some general report of what they had discussed in each session in case I was asked. The requirements for papers were the same as before. (I never gave exams in these classes.) I had periodic one-to-one conferences with students and I said those would have to continue.

My time with the male students was a continued struggle that never got any better. But the female students came to love their separate sessions. One wrote in her final paper: "Our common bonds as women enabled us to discuss topics with our feelings. We can express our thoughts openly because of the oppression we share. We don't have to *prove* what we say is valid. We trust each woman's words and respect her feelings." Every woman wrote of this experience in glowing terms, including a student who confessed she'd initially been angry at me for not preventing the split.

I've taught on and off for 50 years and I feel I've had a lot of success. But, in a way, the greatest success of my teaching career came in a class where half the students met for half the semester without my being present. My role: I allowed it and supported it.

24 Sexism in a Sports Class

In June 1975 Queens College had its "intersession." Classes would meet for three weeks, five days per week, three hours per day. I had what I thought was a brilliant idea: a class on "The Politics of Sports." It would focus on sports and sexism, sports and racism, sports as a capitalist industry, and the fan pathologies of sports. We would draw on the radical sports movement which began in the late 1960s and on the beginnings of a sociology of sport. This would be one of the first such classes in the U.S.

My hope was that my class would attract lots of men who'd never enroll in a feminist or leftist class. With me as their instructor, with the provocative readings I'd assign, with the outstanding guest speakers I'd invite, they would be exposed to radical perspectives. I wrote a very explicit course description for the catalog. Fifty students enrolled. Had there been a larger room available, I believe we'd have had 150 students.

When I walked into class on the first day, I immediately panicked. What had I done? It felt like walking into a junior high school boys locker room. More than 40 of the 50 students were male. My only strong support came from four courageous feminists, two of whom had taken a previous class with me. We were completely outnumbered. Despite my explicit catalog blurb, it felt like most of the male students had seen the word "sports" and gone into immediate orgasm. Their concept of "the politics of sports" seemed to be whether the New York Yankees should have traded player A for player B.

Toward the end of the first hour, I began speaking of the 1971 baseball World Series. Game Seven, the final game, was played in Pittsburgh. The home team, the Pittsburgh Pirates, was victorious. A huge celebration erupted on the city's streets. It turned into a riot with millions of dollars of property damage. Reports suggested that a good number of women had been raped. When I mentioned those rapes, lots of men in the class laughed. I felt sick. I wanted to leave. I genuinely wanted to walk out the door. But I was the instructor and had to face 44 more class hours with those men over three weeks.

The leader of the conservative forces in the class was a student named Marcus. He was intelligent, outspoken, and argumentative. Politely but strongly, he challenged me, he challenged the guest speakers, he challenged the readings. Always on the issues; never a personal attack.

One of the guest speakers was Pat Del Rey. I'd never met her. I'd heard she was the only woman in the college's Physical Education Department who called herself a feminist. Pat gave an excellent talk on unequal treatment of women in sports. She identified and described many ways in which girls and women faced bias, discrimination, and exclusion. She explored how this contributed to the broader sexism of our culture.

As usual, once time began for questions and comments, Marcus was the first to raise his hand. He explained: "I have to agree with 98 percent of what you've said. Girls just aren't treated fairly in sports. But, well… well… well, to be honest… I'd much rather talk to a girl than play basketball with her."

Pat Del Rey didn't hesitate. She immediately replied: "You know, I have a feeling that there are many women who would rather play basketball with you than talk to you."

All the rough times of that teaching experience were worth it for that moment.

25   The 1977 Blackout

July 13-14, 1977. Major blackout across New York City and elsewhere.

In the mid-1970s, I'd gotten together once in a while with Angela. We'd been high school classmates but had moved in completely different circles. Somehow we discovered we lived blocks from each other on the Upper West Side and connected.

Angela was really nice and I was quite attracted to her. But I was involved in radical politics and she was far more conventional. Our meetings were not "dates" in any sense. There was a nice rapport between us, but even being closer friends seemed out of the question.

On that memorable night, we went for a drink in the neighborhood. Then she invited me back to her apartment, where she lived alone. There had been no flirting of any kind. It simply felt like a comfortable way to talk a little more. I expected nothing. Then the lights went out. We looked out her windows and saw no lights. Obviously, the electricity was out everywhere at least in our neighborhood. From the radio, we quickly learned that the blackout was all over the city.

We continued to talk. Angela had two couches in her living room. She was on one, I was on the other. I felt a stronger connection. I felt a stronger attraction. I wondered if she did as well. I hoped she did. Finally I said, without moving any closer: "I'd really like to hold you."

Sounding a little shocked, Angela said: "But we haven't dated!" I didn't move in a world where that mattered. I'd gotten involved with women where there was never a classic "date." I felt Angela was implicitly acknowledging that the attraction was mutual, but that didn't matter. She needed the official rules to be followed.

We lived blocks away but in different worlds. I had no idea how to respond. The awkward moment was silently pushed away. I went home. And we never saw each other again.

26 The Washcloth

I heard a neighbor screaming in the hall. Once before she'd been hit by her husband and I'd intervened to help her. We'd never spoken about it after the first incident. I'd decided that if she didn't say anything I shouldn't. Now she was out there, crying, and this time bleeding. He'd hit her in the face and she had a cut.

I ran inside and grabbed the first thing I could reach that might help, a green washcloth. I gave it to her and she put it over the cut. Then her husband came out of their apartment. And a male neighbor appeared, having heard the uproar.

I angrily told the husband: "If you do this again, I'm calling the police." He said nothing. The injured woman said nothing. The neighbor who was watching said nothing. The woman and her husband went back inside their home. The silent neighbor—who'd offered no support thus far--again said nothing. He went back inside. The next time I saw my neighbor she made no reference to that night. As before, I felt I shouldn't say anything. And I didn't.

I never got my washcloth back. Not that this loss was a problem for me. But I kept thinking about that washcloth. It had to have been awful for my neighbor to look at that reminder of that hideous night. She knew it wasn't hers. She couldn't return it without acknowledging what had happened, including my involvement. I have to believe that she threw it away as soon as possible.

27 <u>The Distance</u>

One afternoon in late 1980 my father came over to see me. He was 78 years old, close to 79. I was 33. He sat on my living room couch; I sat in a chair facing him. We were talking, nothing special. Suddenly I looked at him as I never had before. I got teary. I hadn't cried in front of my father since I was a boy. I was completely shocked.

At first he didn't seem to realize that I was crying. Then he finally sensed something was wrong and asked. I replied: "I was... I was just looking at you...I was realizing that you're old... that one of these days... you're going to die... and... I'll really miss you." I couldn't believe what was happening. I'd never said anything like that to my father. Nothing within a mile of that.

He was almost nonchalant. He said "Well, we've all got to die sometime!" Then—it seemed incredible at the time—he completely changed the subject. He said "I was thinking about when I was a boy and Uncle Robert came to visit. He brought those Indian artifacts." (I was named after my great-uncle, an early German Jewish immigrant who'd fought for the North in the Civil War.)

My father couldn't cope with what had happened. It was obvious. I was profoundly hurt. But, days later, even before I spoke to my therapist, I realized that what I'd done was wonderful. Even if he couldn't stay with me then, even if he had to shut down the conversation, it was great that I'd cried in front of him. That I'd said what I had. If he died the next day, the next year, whenever, he'd heard me say that.

He lived another 4½ years. Inspired by what I'd somehow done that day, I kept at it. I became more open with him both with my words and by touching him. Eventually he began responding in kind, both verbally and physically. We became much closer. It all began on that crucial day.

In his last years, my father almost died from a heart attack, then almost died from pneumonia, then had repeated incidents of congestive heart failure that sent him to the hospital. It was obvious his time was running out. In 1985, he had another round of congestive heart failure and ended up in the Cardiac Care Unit of Lenox Hill Hospital. Almost immediately, the doctors told my mother and myself that by their usual measures they didn't understand why he was still alive. They actually said that!

I knew why. His 83rd birthday, on March 18th, was only a few days away. I was certain he wouldn't die before his birthday—and he didn't. I brought in a birthday cake and lit 84 candles—a complete violation of hospital safety policies. It was the last day in which he had periods where he was really himself, lucid and conversational. He died on March 24th. He'd proven me right.

28 Saying Goodbye

Though it was decades ago, I can still recall the shock. It was my first morning home on the Upper West Side after a summer visit to London. As I had day after day for many years, I went to buy a morning paper at my favorite news-stand on 79th Street and Broadway. But I was soon shaken out of my slumber: the newsstand had vanished.

As a result, I never got to say goodbye to Joel, the co-owner. Joel who had long been a fixture in my morning routine. Joel, who called me "Bobby," which virtually no one had since I was a teenager at summer camp.

Life in New York is profoundly enriched by the relationships many of us establish in our neighborhoods or near our jobs with people who aren't quite friends. My connection to Joel was a good example. I saw him five or six mornings a week, we mainly talked about sports, but here and there we had longer and deeper conversations. We didn't share our last names or phone numbers, and there were lots of important things we didn't ask or tell each other. But he was always warm and kind, and knowing him had real meaning for me.

Joel had mentioned the strain of his long hours on the job, but had given no indication that he and his partner were about to give up their business. Then, suddenly, he was gone. Some nearby shopkeepers confirmed that the stand had been closed, but no one knew how to reach

Joel. If I had made a determined effort, I probably could have found his phone number. But calling him might have been awkward and surely wouldn't have been the same as a face-to-face farewell. So I did nothing—except think of him whenever I saw that corner of Broadway barren without a newsstand. When such relationships end and we never get to say goodbye, it's as if these ties didn't really matter. But they did. They do.

A few years later, history seemed to be repeating itself. This time it involved wonderful, dignified, soft-spoken Mr. Ortiz, who fixed my television set and turntable for over a decade. One sunny afternoon I took a stroll on Amsterdam Avenue and abruptly discovered that his repair shop had been boarded up. I inquired next door and learned that Mr. Ortiz had retired. Again, it seemed there would be no closure. But, months later, I was walking in the neighborhood and there he was! I was thrilled to see him, we had a lovely chat, and for once the ending felt right.

It didn't end as well with Eleni, a young woman from Greece who was working evening shifts with her boyfriend at a diner near my home. It was mainly a breakfast and lunch place, rarely busy on weekday evenings; as a result, the two of them occasionally passed the time by playing chess. Eventually, I began playing with Eleni, who was just learning the game. But she improved so quickly, so dramatically, that I realized I might never beat her again. Eleni remained gracious and modest as her victories mounted.

I was saved from endless defeats only because her boss banned the staff from any further chess games.

One night I noticed some strangers looking over the restaurant. Eleni was at the cash register; she seemed relaxed and we shared our hope that her boss would soon lift the ban against chess. The very next morning, on a short visit for breakfast, I came across a surprising scene. The waiters and cashiers were all new; it soon became clear that the business had been sold.

Eleni never returned. I suspect that her boss kept her in the dark, and that only at the very end of their shift were Eleni and her boyfriend informed that their jobs were over. So I never got to say a final "thank you" for all those chess games and conversations.

The richness of our city isn't just our families, our friends, our co-workers, and the great artists, athletes, or actors whose genius we may get to see. It's also our day-to-day interactions with the people we get to know as they sell us the newspaper, as they fix our TV, as they bring us food in a favorite restaurant.

We remember them, even when we never get to say goodbye.

29 Does Success Change People?

In the early 1980s, I wrote celebrity interviews and profiles for newspapers. Some with authors, some with performers. Among those I met with were cartoonist and playwright Jules Feiffer, essayist (especially on baseball) Roger Angell, folksinger Mary Travers, and actors Howard Rollins and Louise Lasser.

I'd loved Mary Steenburgen's early films, especially her Oscar-winning performance in *Melvin and Howard.* Howard Rollins, who'd become a dear friend, had worked with Mary in *Ragtime* and raved about her. In late 1983, she had two films about to open. I met with her for an hour in her room at the famed Carlyle Hotel in Manhattan. At one point, her then-husband, Malcolm McDowell, wandered into the room in a bathrobe. They both looked gorgeous.

Mary told me that she had been "the first hippie in Little Rock." Because of her Arkansas ties, she later became good friends with Bill and Hillary Clinton. She'd had a meteoric rise. She'd been a struggling actress in New York City, waitressing at an East Village restaurant called The Magic Pan and getting an occasional off-off-Broadway gig. Her friends were struggling actors, just like her.

One day Mary went to the office of an agent. The large reception room was filled with actors waiting for auditions and meetings. In walked Jack Nicholson. She watched him go into an office, but not the office of the agent Mary was expecting to see. Soon thereafter Mary was unexpectedly called into the meeting with Nicholson. He was preparing to do the film *Goin' South* and wanted her to read some lines. She did. He flew her out to Hollywood at his own expense for a screen test. She got the role; it was her first film. Two years later, she won her Oscar. In virtually no time, she'd gone from being one of 10,000 aspiring actresses doing waitressing jobs to Hollywood stardom.

In my research for the profile, I'd read that Mary's meteoric rise hadn't gone over so well with some of her struggling actor friends. I wanted to ask her about this, but knew it would be delicate. After about half an hour, I brought up the subject very carefully. I said: "I don't want to push you into a conversation you don't want to have…." She interrupted me. Nicely but forcefully, she said: "You couldn't!"

Mary continued and said she'd comment, but only briefly. She verified that some people had said she "had changed." She acknowledged: "Of course I've changed in certain ways. The conditions of my life have changed." Then she added pointedly: "People always talk about how success changes people. And it can. But what they never say is that *lack of success* also changes people." Of the many, many interviews I've done in my life—both on social science projects and as a journalist—this was the most powerful moment.

There was a telling postscript. I interviewed Mary on a weekday morning. That Friday she had two films coming out. One was *Cross Creek,* a biopic about the novelist Marjorie Kinnan Rawlings. Mary had the lead role, Malcom McDowell was in it, and it was the film that set off Alfre Woodard's great career. (Woodard was nominated for an Oscar for Best Supporting Actress.) The other film was *Romantic Comedy,* a romantic comedy in which Mary starred opposite Dudley Moore.

On the morning I met with Mary, she was literally at the top of the Hollywood A-list for actresses. Then Friday came. The critics gave *Cross Creek* a mixed reception and it did poorly at the box office. They trashed *Romantic Comedy* and it almost immediately disappeared from theaters.

Just days after I met intelligent, impressive Mary Steenburgen, her career was never the same. She dropped off the top of the A-list. She's worked steadily ever since and has given lots of outstanding performances. But never again was she where she was on the day I interviewed her. What a business!

30 <u>Liberating Mary</u>

No visit to London can really begin for me until I go to the National Portrait Gallery, near Trafalgar Square, and pay my respects to a lovely painting of Mary Wollstonecraft that I helped "liberate" from the museum's "dungeons."

The seeds of my rescue began in the late 1970s, when I visited the gallery but couldn't find a painting of Wollstonecraft. A few years earlier, my men's study group on early feminist literature had devoted six months to the life and work of the inspiring English writer of the late 18th century, best known for *A Vindication of the Rights of Woman.* I subsequently lectured at women's studies classes about this eloquent crusader who offered challenging political insights and was bold enough to attack in print some of the most famous men of her time, among them Burke, Rousseau, and Talleyrand.

Because of my great admiration for Wollstonecraft, she was on my mind when I walked through the National Portrait Gallery and then stopped at the gift shop. In a most unlikely place—the "G" section of the postcards—I suddenly recognized a postcard of her labeled "Mary Godwin (nee Wollstonecraft)." In her 30s, Wollstonecraft had married the British philosopher William Godwin but had continued to use and write under her own name. The National Portrait Gallery either hadn't noticed or didn't approve.

The postcard indeed featured a portrait of Wollstonecraft, but where was the painting itself? At the information desk, I learned that the portrait (by John Opie, circa 1797) was currently housed in the storage area. The gallery's walls included few paintings of women—most of whom were best known for some biological or romantic connection to a famous man. At the same time, there was apparently no room for a portrait of England's feminist pioneer.

The story might have ended there, but the woman at the information desk volunteered that a visitor could request to see any painting not on display. The timing was right, a guard was found, and I was soon down in a storage room standing before Opie's striking portrait.

The painting shows Wollstonecraft in simple clothing: a black beret and a loose white blouse—without any of the lacy feminine frills of that era. She seems intelligent, serene, hardly the dangerous radical so vilified by her enemies. Against a dark background, a single light source brilliantly illuminates Wollstonecraft's face and blouse, as if the artist saw Wollstonecraft's burning feminist spirit as a beacon of truth amidst the prejudice and ignorance around her.

During visits to London over the next few years, I retraced those steps to see Opie's portrait and lamented that others wouldn't get that opportunity. In early 1984, however, I quite literally encountered an obstacle. A guard said I couldn't see the painting because there was "something in the way." The assistant registrar, Andrea Gall, was called in and countered: "So let's move it!" We did, and as we admired the portrait together, we wondered why it was not on display.

The time had come to protest Wollstonecraft's imprisonment. I requested a meeting with Jacob Simon, the new curator for the gallery's 18th century collection. When we spoke in his office, I urged him to find room for the painting and to label it just as she is remembered, Mary Wollstonecraft. He was polite but noncommittal.

Later that year, Mr. Simon sent me a carefully worded letter stating that the Wollstonecraft portrait would soon go on display—but only for four months, to take the place of a painting of Wordsworth on loan to another museum. Thrilling as this news was, I was also saddened because I wouldn't be in London again during those months and thus would never see the fruits of my protest. Then, shortly thereafter, I learned that the portrait had been cleaned, given an impressive new frame, and was now hanging for all to see... under the name of Mary Wollstonecraft.

Now I regretted even more that I'd never see the portrait on the gallery's walls. But when the Wordsworth painting returned to its home in early 1985, I received stunning news and Jacob Simon became a true hero. Despite his original plan, he never took down the portrait of Wollstonecraft and she has remained on display ever since.

She can be found today in a small room with stained wooden floors, along with portraits of her husband, William Godwin, and their daughter, Mary Shelley. (Wollstonecraft died in 1797 shortly after giving birth to the younger Mary, best known as the author of *Frankenstein.*) Wollstonecraft and her loved ones look out proudly on an illustrious array of companions: Percy Shelley, Wordsworth, Keats, Byron, Coleridge, Blake, and Austen.

Virginia Woolf wrote of Wollstonecraft: "One form of immortality is hers undoubtedly: she is alive and active, she argues and experiments, we hear her voice and trace her influence even now among the living."

And, I'm delighted to say, we see her portrait as well.

• •

Thanks to the efforts of Mary on the Green—led by feminists from London, with supporters from Britain and other countries—there is a glorious postscript to this article. In late 2020, a sculpture memorial honoring Mary Wollstonecraft—done by a female sculptor, Maggi Hambling—was unveiled and dedicated in London's Newington Green. That's where Wollstonecraft ran a school for girls in the late 1700s.

31 Bailey's Irish Cream

I first visited Edinburgh as a college student in the summer of 1968. Went for a weekend with friends and loved it. Didn't get back there till July 1985. I knew no one in Scotland. Took a night train from London, arrived at the Edinburgh train station, and booked a room in a bed-and-breakfast place.

Before I left the train station, I saw a little shop that made T-shirts to order. I wanted to get one for a friend in the U.S. Began a really nice conversation with the young woman working in the shop. She'd just graduated from a university and wanted to become a physical education teacher. But there were no teaching jobs of any kind to be had.

She mentioned that a terrific outdoor track meet with lots of international stars was on that night in a local stadium. I'd never seen a track meet in person and had always wanted to do so. She said I'd better get in a cab and go immediately to the stadium to buy a ticket because the meet might sell out. It seemed crazy. My first night in Edinburgh and I'm going to go to track meet? But I knew no one in town and had no evening plans. So why not go?

I tore off to the stadium and found the line to buy tickets. Next to us was a map of the stadium. I had no idea what the stadium was really like or where it was good to sit at a track meet. As I stared at the map, so did the man behind me.

We got into a lovely conversation. Jon was a physician who worked for the National Health Service. He ran marathons and loved track and field. He'd visited New York and raved about my town. He was taking his wife and their two young children to the meet.

We were now close to the ticket window. Since I was in front of Jon, I'd be buying my ticket first. Inspired by our terrific chat, I was a bit bold. I said: "Look, I'm here alone. Would it be OK if I sat with you and your family?" I felt nervous asking, but this was exactly the kind of risk taking I'd had in mind on that night at Yale when I realized I was boring.

Jon got *very* excited. He said: "That would be wonderful! I was going to ask you, but I thought perhaps you were going with other people." He said he couldn't pick me up at my bed-and-breakfast place because he lived on the other side of town and had to get his family. But that after the meet I'd have to come back to their home and have drinks with him and his wife. And eventually he'd drive me back to where I was staying. He was incredibly welcoming.

We got five tickets together and I met them at the seats. The track meet was exciting but for a frightening moment. Zola Budd, a 19-year-old white South African distance runner, was competing. There were protests from local anti-apartheid activists. Then, when Budd—who was quite small and slight—was in the midst of her race, a guy from the crowd ran onto the track and after her. No doubt she was terrified!

Fortunately, he didn't do any harm when he got near her. After the meet, we went back to Jon and Judy's home and we began talking and drinking. Jon asked if I liked Bailey's Irish Cream. I had no idea what it was. He said I had to try some, I loved it, and I've loved it ever since.

When it was very late, we somehow discovered that all three of us were devoted fans of Tom Lehrer, a mathematician from the U.S. who became quite popular in the 1960s with satirical songs he'd written and performed while at the piano. Some were very political, brilliant, and hilarious. I had no idea that anyone in the U.K. knew who he was, but a show of his music had been a big hit on London's West End. We drank Bailey's Irish Cream and together sang out loud many Tom Lehrer songs.

Eventually Jon and Judy kindly hosted me during two summers so I could see the spectacular Edinburgh Fringe Festival. We were friends for decades. They're both gone now, but I keep Bailey's Irish Cream on my kitchen table and it reminds me of that very special first night at their home.

32 <u>More Time for Healing</u>

It all began when a fence collapsed, fell out of the sky, and hit me on the head.

Hurricane Gloria had descended on Manhattan early on September 27, 1985. That afternoon, with the storm seemingly over and the sun shining brightly, I headed downtown with my friend Alice. Near Washington Square Park, we passed a five-story building with a wooden fence on the penthouse. Perhaps weakened by the hurricane, the fence fell apart and large pieces of wood crashed to the ground.

I never saw what hit me. Alice escaped injury, but I was struck on the head and the back of the neck. I was down on the ground, unconscious, a bloody mess. At first, Alice thought I was dead. When I regained consciousness, I was delirious and agitated. As EMS workers placed me on a stretcher to take me to St. Vincent's Hospital, I screamed at Alice: "Don't let them take me away!"

I have no idea how long I was delirious. I have no memory of being on the ground after the fence collapsed, no memory of being in an ambulance, no memory of entering the hospital. Suddenly there I was in what I realized must be an emergency room. A male doctor was asking me questions that would be asked of anyone who'd had a serious head injury. Perhaps he'd already asked 10 times. He asked if I knew my name and could say it. I did. He asked if I knew what city we were in. I did. He

103

asked if I knew who was the president of the United States. It was 1985 and a terrible actor from Hollywood was in the White House. I answered: "Unfortunately, yes." That was the moment when I knew I was myself again, whatever the injuries and the road ahead.

I stayed in the hospital for 10 days. My skull and one vertebrae of my neck were fractured. I had a concussion, cuts on my head which required stitches, and an ugly black eye. Most seriously, I had an internal tear that could open the way for bacteria to pass from the sinuses to the brain area. The doctors kept me flat for six days—I wasn't allowed to raise my head from my pillow—and the tear healed and closed. As a result, I avoided delicate neurosurgery.

My most shattering time at St. Vincent's came near the end when I was finally strong enough to take a shower. I joyously turned on the water, only to confront an unexpected horror: my hair was thickly matted with dried blood. I began to cry, and my tears reached an avalanche as I realized how much blood there was, how long it would take to wash it out of my hair.

The memories of that blood, and all that it symbolized, stayed with me long after I left the hospital. I didn't need to focus endlessly on my accident: I treasured going to baseball games and escapist movies more than before. But it still felt crucial to talk now and then about the chilling experience that I'd survived.

A few people were wonderfully supportive and sensitive, but many others put up walls, especially once they learned I was on the way to recovery. Some never asked about my feelings and changed the subject whenever I mentioned the accident. Others avoided me entirely: they didn't call or visit when I was in the hospital or even afterward.

When I was home recovering and called one out-of-town friend to tell her what had happened, she quickly cut me off and asked: "So how's the rest of your life?" (At that moment, I was far from 100 percent better; recuperating *was* my life.) Then I didn't hear from her again for more than a year.

Our society seems to enforce a statute of limitations on permissible reactions to trauma; in effect, an unspoken time limit for recovery. People who experience physical or emotional pain are allowed a week or two—at most, a month—to be upset. They can be sad, terrified, enraged; they can do bizarre things that will be ignored or excused. But once that brief period has passed, then they're supposed to be "over" the experience. And they're expected—not by everyone, but by too many—to shut up about it.

Consequently, as people block off meaningful discussions (often unconsciously) with those who have suffered, we hurt friends and family members when they are most vulnerable.

Someone I know had a serious operation and needed to wear a cast for six months. Because her surgeons did such a good job, she was left with only a small scar. But she recalls wishing she had a large and glaring scar, so that people would realize what a long and torturous process she had been through.

We all have deep scars, whether visible or not. Even when our dried blood is washed away, it is still there with us. We need caring, warmth, support, and time to make a genuine recovery from the long-term damage of trauma. How can we abolish the statute of limitations and help each other with the essential work of healing?

33 **Picked Last But Proud**

I always feel a certain sadness as spring approaches, for my volleyball game is no more.

My adult volleyball days began on a sunny May afternoon in 1986. As I strolled around Central Park's Great Lawn near the Delacorte Theater, I spied a woman and a group of men in the midst of what seemed a low-key, thoroughly enjoyable session of volleyball. They invited me to join them and I did… for six or seven years. Many of the regulars were performers who had originally met through summer stock and a good number were gay.

We met every Saturday from May through September. Our game was far from textbook volleyball. For example, we had a cherished tradition of letting newcomers serve a few times till they got it over the net. Even for the rest of us, any serve that hit the net and went over led to a second serve—again in defiance of normal volleyball rules.

The rules, in fact, were a constant subject of derision. Anyone calling out a minor infraction would have been mocked unmercifully, and it wasn't hard to see why. Although some of our regulars were terrific athletes, many of us—female or male, gay or straight—had been childhood victims of callous jocks and gym teachers. It was generally unspoken, but you could feel it.

Our most memorable volleyball moment came on a hot summer day. Although about a third of our regular players were female, that afternoon only men were playing when two women wandered by and stopped to watch. As usual, someone encouraged them to join us, but they insisted they simply wanted to observe. It was obvious that this wasn't true, that they were dying to play but were nervous about entering our male enclave. We kept asking, they kept declining.

Finally, one of the men yelled out: "Listen, you have to understand: this is the kind of game you're only allowed to join if you're the kind of person who was always picked last!" The women exploded in laughter, as we all did, and they immediately entered the game. And one of them proved a far better player than any man there.

In its early years, our volleyball game had a consistently wonderful, playful feel. In that spirit, we held a raucous annual winter party where each participant was assured of receiving some outrageous award. Indeed, my friend Dick, who had visited one summer from London and had played volleyball for the first time in his life, was later thrilled to receive an award for "Best Player from a Monarchy."

There were sad times as well. On one Saturday in the late 1980s, Gordon and I were the only players who showed up. Since there was no game, I walked him back to his subway stop and we had a really nice talk. Only weeks later, I was stunned to hear that Gordon was in the hospital, gravely ill due to AIDS. When I visited him, he could barely see or hear me, and he died soon after.

As the 1980s ended, our game began to change. New players joined, more serious players. The level of volleyball improved, but the atmosphere deteriorated. Now people talked endlessly about their volleyball leagues and complained when we didn't enforce standard rules. Soon our tradition of giving a player an extra serve came under fire and then it was gone. I eventually had to face the truth: this was no longer the volleyball game I'd loved. It was turning into exactly the kind of game I'd always avoided.

Like many of the original regulars, I began coming less often. Soon our game officially died. Sometime later, I went to an informal volleyball game at a neighborhood school—supposedly open to newcomers—where I found myself in trouble right away. As an example, they always passed from anywhere in the middle line to the center person on the front line, but no one had the decency to explain this. They simply glared at me until I figured it out.

I left in disgust and thought back to that day in Central Park when those two women joined us. I guess I miss volleyball, but what I really miss is being part of a game that genuinely welcomed everyone—including those accustomed to being picked last.

34 <u>A Lesson Playing Poker</u>

My parents, my grandmother, and my aunts were all card players. Especially canasta, which I quickly learned and loved. I played pinochle with my father. I played casino, poker, gin rummy, hearts, many versions of solitaire, lots of card games. Loved them all. Never for gambling, just for the joy of the games.

At about age 40, a friend told me of a low-stakes poker game at the Hell's Kitchen home of a theater stage manager. It was on Monday nights when Broadway theaters were closed. I decided to check it out. Aya had two tables going simultaneously. Very low stakes. Many of the players were young actors and crew. It was always dealer's choice. The popular poker variations used there included lots of wild cards or other complicated rules. I found it difficult just to know what was actually a good hand.

Those Monday nights were great fun. But, over time, I became intellectually enchanted by poker. I wanted to understand the game, I wanted to get better, I read a book or two—and I started winning consistently against Aya's friends. Mainly by following a very simple rule: if your initial cards are terrible, you have to fold. Don't keep betting in the hope that your later cards will be brilliant. Just wait for the next hand.

One of the regulars, Carson, was an actor in his mid 50s. We hit it off, in good part because each of us was frustrated with the bizarre poker games popular at Aya's. Eventually Carson decided to begin a new poker game at his home. One table, maximum of seven players, people he carefully invited. Only four poker variations allowed, dealer's choice: draw poker, five-card stud, seven-card stud, and seven card high-low. Wild cards completely banned. The stakes were a bit higher than at Aya's, but still quite reasonable. Over three or four hours, you could perhaps win or lose $50 maximum but that was quite unusual. More likely you'd win or lose $10 to $25.

I played at Carson's home for a few months. These were better players than at Aya's, but I was still winning most of the time. I started to get excited, thinking "I've become a really good poker player!"

Carson called one night. Some guys he knew were having their weekly game in a few days. Two of the regulars couldn't come and he'd been asked to fill in. The stakes would be a bit higher than at his game—an ante of $1--but not ridiculous. Did I want to join him? I said "Sure."

I brought $50 in cash. Everyone was quite friendly. We began and I had a run of mediocre cards. Mainly I did the right thing: folding right away if my initial cards were lousy. I stayed in a few hands but lost apart from one high-low game where I split the pot. After an hour, my entire $50 was gone.

I hadn't played poorly. I really hadn't. I knew if I stayed it wasn't likely that I'd get such lousy cards all night. I was certain that no one was cheating. But over that hour it had become clear that these guys were simply better players than I was. If I spent 10 nights playing poker with them, I'd end up a loser at least seven or eight of those nights.

I told them I was very sorry. I'd brought $50, I'd lost it all, and I needed to leave. They said "Don't worry about that!" They offered to advance me more money. I restrained myself from laughing. I could see that I was out of my league; surely they could see that as well. Of course they were willing to advance me more money! I politely declined and headed home.

It was extremely embarrassing, But even before I got home that night I realized I'd been incredibly lucky. I'd spent $50 learning a valuable lesson that could have cost me *so* much more. I'd thought I was becoming a really good poker player. Now, $50 lighter, I realized that self-praise was absurd.

Years later, I was on a cruise that had a game room with card tables and machines. A staff member was dealing poker and anyone could join. I was playing against two or three guys and winning. Then a new guy sat down at the table. I quickly realized he was a better poker player than I was. No false vanity this time. I finished a hand, took my reduced winnings, and left. My embarrassing $50 lesson was paying dividends!

35 Howard Rollins

In 1982, I went to see Milos Forman's film adaptation of *Ragtime.* I hadn't read E.L. Doctorow's acclaimed novel. All I knew was that *Ragtime* was set in the early 20th century and was a sprawling novel combining fictional and real-life characters (among the latter, Harry Houdini, Emma Goldman, J.P. Morgan, and Booker T. Washington).

As I began watching, I was soon mesmerized by an actor completely unfamiliar to me. Howard Rollins was playing Coalhouse Walker, Jr., a ragtime pianist who becomes a target of racism. He is shocked, then outraged, demands justice, and becomes increasingly angry and rebellious. When, inevitably, he is merci-lessly gunned down by police—even though his hands are clearly raised in the air in surrender—I felt I died a little with that character. Never could I have guessed how I'd feel in late 1996 when it was Howard Rollins who died, not Coalhouse Walker, Jr.

Rollins was universally praised for his performance. He was nominated for an Oscar for Best Supporting Actor at a time when African Americans were almost never honored that way because they so rarely were given roles that might bring a nomination. Among his films after *Ragtime* was the lead in Norman Jewison's film, *A Soldier's Story,* drawn from Charles Fuller's Pulitzer-prize winning play. Howard later starred in the TV series *In the Heat of the Night* with Carroll O'Connor.

I'd begun doing celebrity interviews for the *Los Angeles Herald Examiner,* at that time the #2 newspaper in L.A. I was mainly interviewing authors, but I proposed Howard Rollins to my editor, my friend Susan Christian Goulding, and she gave her OK. It turned out that Howard lived six blocks from me on the Upper West Side. He came to my home for what I'd expected would be an hour, but we talked for three hours.

By the end, it was obvious that we would be friends. Part of it came from a surprising response to a predictable question. I asked Howard what it had been like growing up in Baltimore. His response was "It happened to lie south of Canada." Many white journalists wouldn't have understood what he was saying. I knew that Malcolm X had famously stated that anywhere south of Canada was the South! Another part of our initial connection, I believe, came from a choice I made. *Ragtime* was James Cagney's last film; in some interviews people were more interested in asking Howard about Cagney than his own life and work. So in three hours I never once mentioned the name James Cagney.

Early on, I realized that this brilliant actor was a wonderful but troubled soul. Our friendship seemed to be going fine, but one night on the phone Howard told me we couldn't be friends anymore. It came out of nowhere; we'd never had a disagreement. I was stunned. He told me he couldn't be friends with anyone. He went out of his way to speak glowingly of me and insist that this wasn't about me. I believed him. His words were kind and caring but unyielding. It was profoundly sad. About a year later, I ran into Howard in our neighborhood. He was pleasant, we had a nice chat, but it was obvious that our friendship wasn't going to resume.

I went to London in July 1986. Absolutely by chance, I noticed that a production of Herb Gardner's comedy *I'm Not Rappaport* was on in the West End, with Paul Scofield and Howard Rollins in the lead roles. Howard had the role that Ossie Davis had played on Broadway. The character was supposed to be in his 70s. Davis was 59 at that time. In 1986, Howard was 36.

I knew Howard loved acting on the stage. That's how his career had begun. At 17, he'd accompanied a friend who was auditioning for a production of *Of Mice and Men,* was convinced to audition himself, and was cast. I'd never seen Howard in a play and felt I had to go. Couldn't miss it. I was certain he'd be great.

Then I wondered: should I try to talk with him? I decided I had to make the effort, but I had no idea how he'd react. I came up with a plan. I bought a ticket for a weekday matinee performance. He'd also have an evening show that night. I decided to go *very* early and meet him at the stage door. I'd ask if we could talk in between shows. I hoped he wouldn't have commitments in between.

I got there that day and found the stage door at the back of the theater. And I waited. And waited. I knew Howard would need a lot of makeup to play a character twice his age. He'd need to get there early. But people obviously working on the show were coming to the stage door and going inside. It was getting closer to showtime. Looked like Howard was late.

Then I saw him two blocks away. At that time, central London was very white. Howard was tall and had dark skin. He was wearing a fur coat, looking at his watch, shaking his head. Obviously I'd been right: he was late. The moment of truth was ahead.

Finally he saw me. And let out a HUGE scream!!! He was completely stunned and seemed thrilled to see me. And freaked out because he was late. I told him I was seeing the matinee and asked if we could talk in his dressing room right after the show. He said "yes." But he was panicky about going inside and getting ready. Before he could leave, I said: "You've *got* to do something for me. Once you step inside this door, be sure to give them my name. So when I return here after the show they'll know you actually want to see me, that I'm not a groupie."

I liked the show and Howard was, of course, superb. I returned to the stage door and fortunately they had my name. I met Howard in his dressing room. We talked and talked. After that we were close friends till the day he died.

36 The World's Most Jealous Sports Fan

In the early 1980s, I had an interview for a teaching job at a program where the students were members of a labor union. I was questioned by a really nice guy named Jason, it went well, but I wasn't hired.

Some years later, I ran into Jason on my block on the Upper West Side. Turned out he and his wife lived just up the street. He remembered me and we had a lovely chat. I saw him on the block quite a few times after that and it was always pleasant. Then I stopped seeing him.

I'd met someone at a poker game who, like me, was a fan of the New York Mets. She had a Sunday season ticket plan and it sounded great. I bought a plan: two tickets for all Sunday home games, about 15 per season. Not prime seats, but decent seats. The cost was reasonable. It included an option for some but not all postseason games. I kept that plan for most of a decade.

As a result, I was in Shea Stadium for the magical Game Six of the 1986 World Series. Not in my usual Sunday seats—the plan didn't allow that for postseason games—but instead high and way back in right field. The Mets were one out away from being eliminated by the Boston Red Sox, but made a dramatic 10th inning comeback, culminating in a ground ball by Mookie Wilson that went through first baseman Bill Buckner's legs. The Mets had an impossible victory and in Game Seven they won the World Series.

Sometime in the summer of 1987 I was walking alone in Central Park, right near Belvedere Castle and the Great Lawn, and there was Jason. I was delighted to see him and vice versa. He said he and his wife had split up and that's why he was no longer on West 79th Street. As we were catching up, we discovered that we were both passionate fans of the Mets. I said with excitement: "I was at Game Six!" Immediately, without a word, Jason turned around and walked away. Just left me standing there.

Why this abrupt and shocking departure? I can only imagine one explanation: he was intensely jealous that I was at that game and he wasn't. Given his reaction, you'd have thought I'd stolen his ticket! And if he concluded I was some corporate fat cat who had gotten great seats without even paying for them, none of that was true. I had lousy seats and I *had* paid for them.

I've never seen Jason again. But whenever Game Six is mentioned, I think of him. He's probably still angry that I was there.

37 <u>Perjury in New Orleans</u>

In 1988, I went to New Orleans for the first time. The only person I knew there was a former student of mine from Yale. Flora was now working as an assistant district attorney. Days before my arrival, she said she might not be able to see me because a very important rape trial on which she was working was about to begin.

As it turned out, we were able to have dinner on the night of my arrival. The trial was beginning the very next morning. I thought it might be interesting to see her in court. I had plenty of free time ahead, so I asked if I could come and she said that was fine. I intended to arrive midmorning, stay for an hour, then have lunch and begin my sightseeing. In the end, I was mesmerized by the trial and stayed right through to the verdict at 8:00 p.m.

A young, white, middle-class woman had been raped. She was working as a legal assistant at a local law firm and was heading to law school. She'd been at a party at someone's home, had run into a former boyfriend, and had gone outside with him to talk. They were sitting in his car together. They were or weren't smoking marijuana. (This was disputed in court.) They were or weren't making out. (Also disputed.) She had a new boyfriend who wasn't at the party.

While they were in the car, a white guy approached them, said he was a cop, and flashed a badge. He asked them to step outside the car, questioned Donald, then questioned Anne. He asked her to get into his car and sit in the passenger seat. He got inside and took off. He drove her to an abandoned parking lot, threatened her with a knife, and raped her. He left her there. He wasn't a cop; his badge was phony.

In many rape cases, it's the woman's word against the man's, sometimes with no physical evidence that can be tied to the attack. In this case, there was a mountain of testimony and physical evidence. There was Anne's testimony and Donald's confirmation of the rapist's pretense to be a police officer. There was Anne's testimony about the rape. A neighbor of the rapist testified that she'd seen him that very day with a knife similar to the one Anne had described. And there was stunning testimony from a friend of the rapist. He'd visited the accused man in jail where the rapist had asked him to lie and provide a phony alibi for that night.

I watched these prosecution witnesses testify. The case seemed overwhelming. The defense attorney's efforts to show that Anne and Donald were smoking marijuana, that they were having secret and improper sex in the car, were pathetic. It seemed certain that the jury would find the defendant guilty. The prosecution rested its case. Then, in a shocker, the rapist took the stand. It was impossible to imagine what he'd say after hearing those four very convincing witnesses.

Remarkably, the rapist went through every detail of the accusations and denied all of it. Anne was lying. Donald was lying. His neighbor was lying. His friend was lying. It was as if they all had grievances against him and were part of a conspiracy—even though of the four only Anne and Donald actually knew each other.

Here's the truly astonishing part: the rapist was *very* convincing. If he'd been the first witness rather than the last, he'd have had a lot of impact. It was scary to imagine how easily he'd persuaded Anne and Donald that he was a cop. I'd never seen a sociopath brilliantly, chillingly spin a web of lies in person. Fortunately, he wasn't the first witness; he was the last.

The jury went out to deliberate. I asked a bailiff how long these conferences usually took. He suggested it would be a good while, at least an hour or two. Instead, the jury returned after 20 minutes. Their verdict was guilty. They must have immediately voted without any discussion.

Earlier, I'd had a nervous lunch with Flora, one of the other D.A.s, and Anne. After the verdict, we went out and celebrated. Justice isn't always blind.

38 The E.R. Doctor

Late 1992. My mother's friend Jean called. My mother—late 70s, some health problems but nothing immediately dangerous—collapsed at lunch. EMS workers arrived quickly but couldn't revive her. I'd better get to Lenox Hill Hospital as soon as possible.

I found Jean in the emergency room. She was about my mother's age. One of her husbands had previously dropped dead right in front of her. She, my mother, and some friends had been at lunch in a restaurant. My mother complained of a shoulder pain. Suddenly she lost consciousness.

We sat there. No one came. Eventually someone appeared and said they were still working on my mother. She'd been in there for a good while. I felt this was ominous. Time passed. Now we were told they'd bring us inside. A doctor would talk to us.

We sat in a room. A physician came, probably a resident on a shift at the emergency room. He introduced himself. He asked if I was Mrs. Lamm's son. I confirmed that. He asked if she'd been complaining of any pains. I said "no." Any recent shortages of breath? I said "no." Has she had any recent history of…?

I interrupted him. "Excuse me, but can you tell me if my mother is still alive?" He paused. "I'm very sorry," he said. "We did all we could do."

I was as angry as I've ever been. How many questions would he have asked before finally telling us that my mother was dead?

I made an instant decision. I was an only child, my father was gone. Jean had watched my mother die right in front of her, just as her husband had. This guy deserved an explosion from me, but I had a lot to deal with. I resolved not to blast away at him. We went through one or two more questions, then he said a social worker would be in to see us. He left.

When the social worker arrived, I told her exactly what had just happened. I said: "I know it must be difficult to tell loved ones that someone has died. But in his position you simply have to do it. You can't put people through torturous questioning that isn't going to change anything." It was obvious that she understood. I urged her to speak with him. I can only hope that she did.

39 <u>Drama on the Softball Field</u>

June 1993. I'm on the softball team of the National Writers Union's New York local. My friend George Robinson is the captain of the team. We play slow-pitch softball in a coed publishers league on Central Park's Great Lawn. I'm a sub, usually as a second baseman or relief pitcher. We have a bad team.

We're playing McGraw-Hill, the company that publishes the sociology textbooks on which I'm a co-author. They're having batting practice. One of their players hits two hard shots, then swings and misses at 12 pitches in a row. It's not easy to miss 12 pitches in a row in slow-pitch softball. People in the field are getting frustrated. I push the McGraw-Hill pitcher to get another batter up there so we can finish batting practice and get the game started.

It's a seven-inning game. No balls and strikes called. Each batter gets three swings. You can take (not swing at) as many pitches as you like. If you hit a foul ball on your final swing or miss entirely, you're out. We get three runs in the top of the first. They quickly tie the score. After five innings, it's 12-12 in a game filled with our many bloop hits and baserunning blunders. At one point, our third base coach sends a runner home who is thrown out by at least ten feet.

I enter the game in the fourth inning. I reach base on an error, then later hit a bases-loaded RBI single. I rarely pitch four innings, but this time I do.

We score five runs in the top of the 6th. We now lead 17-12 and may actually win. I get the first two batters to fly out to our center fielder, one of our best players. Up steps the guy who missed all the pitches in batting practice. He takes lots of pitches, swings and misses, watches many more pitches, swing and misses, take many more pitches, then with his final swing hits a dribbler in front of the plate. I can't get to it in time to get him out at first base. Horribly, this two-out dribbler is the beginning of a six-run inning for McGraw-Hill, assisted by two easy fly balls dropped by our right fielder. Now they've regained the lead, 18-17.

Top of the 7th inning. Our last chance. Our best hitter hits a smash to right center. Looks like a sure home run. As he's running from third base to home plate, he falls down, but somehow scores anyway. Tie score. With two out, we come through in the clutch with three more hits. Now we lead 19-18.

Bottom of the 7th. Our shaky right fielder is still out there along with some subs who are equally unreliable in the field. Eventually there are two out with the tying run on second and the winning run on first.

Who's up? Same guy who took 100 pitches in the previous inning, then hit that dribbler. If I can strike him out, we win. He takes lots of pitches, swings, strike one. Looks at a bunch more, swings, strike two. I'm dying out there, so nervous. Just hoping he'll do something, *anything*, soon. He takes pitch after pitch, finally swings. STRIKE THREE!!! I scream, run off the mound, jump into the catcher's arms.

Final score: National Writers Union 19, McGraw-Hill 18.

40 The Terrible Librarian

I'm a huge admirer of librarians. As a kid, as a college student, as a professional writer, as a college instructor, they've almost always been wonderful and helpful. Many have gone way beyond what seemed reasonable to help me. But there was one....

As a longtime co-author of introductory sociology textbooks for college students, I'd made a serious push beginning in the mid-1980s to get material on disability issues and disability rights into our books. In 1995, we were working on a new edition. As always, I wanted to see if there was new material that would update our disability coverage. I spent an afternoon at the treasured 42nd Street Library and found valuable articles in academic journals, newspapers, and magazines. Alas, two articles from a British journal sounded intriguing but I couldn't find them.

I consulted a reference librarian, who was extremely nice. He checked, then reported that this British journal wasn't in the collection of the 42nd Street Library or anywhere in the New York Public Library system. He told me of a special program of which I was unaware. There was—and still is—an agreement among all the many libraries in New York City: public libraries, university libraries, museum libraries, and other private libraries. If you want to see something that is nowhere in the public library system but is held by a private library of some sort, you can do that. You need a signed form from a librarian for New York Public Library confirming that it's not in their system.

The reference librarian told me that the only place in New York City where I could find that British journal was at Columbia University's science library in Washington Heights. He filled out the required form, signed it, and said to contact them and be ready to present that form.

The next day I called the main number for the science library. A reference librarian answered and gave her name. I explained that I wanted to visit and read those two journal articles. And that I had the proper form signed by the reference librarian at 42nd Street. She bluntly told me that I couldn't use their library. That since I had no connection to Columbia I absolutely couldn't come there.

I was baffled. I repeated exactly what I'd been told at 42nd Street. I had the signed form! She was insistent that I couldn't use the Columbia library and became unpleasant. She offered no assistance of any kind. Finally I asked if there was a supervisor or someone I could speak with. She flatly said there wasn't. By this point I was fuming. I said, "Listen, my name is Bob Lamm. I want you to remember my name. I'm going to come and use your library. You'll see!"

The phone call ended. Half an hour later, I called the same main number. A different reference librarian answered. I asked for the name, title, and mailing address of the library's director. I immediately sent her a letter explaining what had happened at 42nd Street and during my first phone call. I had the name of the awful Columbia librarian. I said that perhaps I had all this wrong, but since I had a signed form I assumed there indeed was such an interlibrary agreement. So I believed I had the right to come to her library and read those articles.

Two days later my phone rang; it was the director of the science library. She was very pleasant and immediately apologized. She said: "I'm sorry, you were right. You can indeed come to our library and read those articles. The only condition is that you can't just show up. You have to make an appointment and bring the signed form." I said that was fine and asked how to do that. She told me to call the same main number I'd previously called.

I consider it a certainty that the director wasn't happy about having to call a stranger and apologize for a reference librarian who'd acted wrongly and callously. No doubt the director had a few things to say to that librarian.

I made the appointment and the next week went to Columbia's science library. I arrived with a plan. I was determined to confront the outrageous librarian, but wanted to be sure I got all my work done before that. Once inside, I went looking for where that librarian's office was. I quickly found it along a wall of small offices for six or seven reference librarians. Her door was open, the light was on, she wasn't inside, but it looked like she was at work that day. I then went into another room, found the journal issues and the articles, took notes, and finished my research.

Now I returned to the librarian's office. This time she was at her desk, door still open. I knocked carefully on the door. She said "Come in!" I put only one foot inside her office. I said "I'm Bob Lamm. I told you I'd come to your library and read those articles. And now I have!"

She exploded. She started screaming at me to get out of her office, even though I really wasn't inside. I just laughed and began to walk toward the exit. About half-way there, I looked back. She was standing outside her door, watching to be sure I was leaving. I just kept smiling and headed out.

I don't live for revenge. It can be extremely destructive to get wrapped up in that emotion. But I'll admit: this time it was very sweet.

41 <u>An Amateur on Stage</u>

I'm not a performer. Never have been. As a ten-year-old at summer camp, I auditioned enthusiastically for *Carousel* and was given two lines. One of them was "Me, too." Nevertheless, I've performed on professional stages three times. And each time I began as an audience member.

I first landed onstage in 1970, when I was just out of college. I went to see *Hair* and was stunned to discover that Jessica Harper was in the cast. I'd met her at Sarah Lawrence two years earlier. Now she was on Broadway and soon she'd be starring in such films as *Stardust Memories, Suspiria,* and *My Favorite Year.* Both before the show and during intermission, cast members stood at the back of the orchestra and I was able to chat with Jessica. At the finale, when the entire cast was dancing and singing "Let The Sunshine In," they motioned for audience members to join them. I got up there, found Jessica, and danced on Broadway.

In the mid-1980s, I fell in love with improv comedy, began taking classes, and did for years. In 1994, I went to see the one-man show *Ricky Jay and His 52 Assistants.* Well known for his work in David Mamet's films, the late Mr. Jay was a genius at performing card tricks and at throwing playing cards as if they were weapons. He was also a remarkable scholar of magic and a historian of confidence games dating back to the Middle Ages.

Well into his brilliant show, Jay explained he was going to teach us how to win lots of money in poker. Imagine that you can control the cards you're dealing, as he seemingly could. If you deal yourself a great hand but all the other players quickly fold, you won't win much money. Consequently, you want to deal everyone an outstanding hand so they'll bet wildly, while being sure to deal yourself the *best* hand.

Jay chose two of us to play poker with him at a card table onstage. The game was five-card draw with no wild cards. He opened a sealed deck and dealt hands to each of us. He'd told us we'd get great hands but nevertheless he'd win. When my turn came, I had four deuces and a nine. Four of a kind! Surely a winning hand in a draw poker game with no wild cards. Jay said "So I guess you'll be standing pat?" (Not exchanging any of my cards for new ones.)

Stand pat? When he'd said we were going to lose? Quite spontaneously, I replied: "Actually, I was hoping for a fifth deuce." The audience laughed heartily, well aware that my fantasy couldn't happen. But Ricky Jay was not amused. He glared at me and growled: "Not in this deck!" Obviously he didn't appreciate some lackey from the audience making a successful, unscripted joke. Nevertheless, I now had one little onstage improv triumph to cherish.

By 2005, I'd somehow become an improv teacher. I went to see a production of *Caligula* at the Classical Theatre of Harlem, with Andre De Shields starring as the infamous

Roman emperor. The show featured exciting dancing, terrific stage fighting, and insane monologues from the incomparable De Shields as the emperor who sleeps with women, men, his sister, children, and animals—and names a horse as the head of the Roman Senate!

During the second act, the cast began filtering through the audience and asking people to join them onstage. Soon about 15 of us were up there dancing with the performers. Then, with no warning, Caligula began cracking a huge whip. His followers ran around terrified; then they rushed Caligula from all sides and (gently) threw him to the ground.

Once De Shields was down, the cast members began stabbing Caligula with imaginary swords and knives. They motioned to the audience members onstage and encouraged us to help kill Caligula. As I endlessly tell my improv students, you've always got to say "yes" and go with what's happening. So I ran up to join in the assassination. Only one problem: I couldn't see Caligula and I wanted to be part of killing the emperor. So I moved around the circle till I could finally see De Shields on the ground and thereby ended up front and center on the stage, with my back to the audience.

The lights were dim as we repeatedly stabbed Caligula. Then I noticed that the cast members on either side of me were slowly sinking to the ground. I wondered if I should do the same; no one had given me any signal. Suddenly

I had a terrifying thought: "What if the lights come on? What if I'm the only one standing… and I'm center stage?"

I got down just in time, for the lights indeed came on. We were all in a circle crouching around the dying emperor. I looked up and was shocked: everyone I could see was a member of the cast. (Only later did I learn that there was one other audience member in the circle.) Now I was really rattled. Was I in the wrong place? Were the actors angry that I was there? I wanted to leave, but I knew I couldn't. If I stood up, I'd distract the audience from the dying Caligula. I had to stay where I was, follow along, and act like I belonged there.

The play continued and finally Caligula died. When the curtain began falling, the cast beckoned for all of us onstage to join them for the curtain call. The audience offered a long, passionate standing ovation and we bowed repeatedly. I was ecstatic! I returned to my seat to retrieve my coat and bag. An audience member—whom I later learned was a professional actor—looked at me and said, "Hey, you were great up there." A little later I met Andre De Shields, he thanked me for joining in, and I told him it was an honor to work with him.

I'm still not a performer, but I've had three memorable evenings onstage. So I encourage everyone: if you're sitting in a theater and a cast member asks you to dance, to play poker, to help kill an emperor, say a huge "yes" and get up there. You won't be sorry!

• •

In 1966, on the night at Yale where I realized I was boring, I decided that I had to begin taking risks, putting myself in uncomfortable situations where I'd meet different kinds of people and would grow as a person. I never dreamed I'd end up as someone who'd teach "The Joy of Improv" comedy classes and workshops for beginners and nonperformers. As someone who'd run workshops using improv and role-playing in serious ways to build skills and to examine sensitive issues.

In the mid-1980s, at a point where I needed something new, I saw a tiny ad in a free community newspaper for a class called "Acting For Fun," obviously an acting class for non-actors. I'd have been too scared to take an acting class with working and aspiring actors, but somehow I decided to give this beginners' class a try. It was mostly improv and I had absolutely no idea what improv was. But we began with a "Mirrors" warmup—a bit like the brilliant mirrors scene in the Marx Brothers' film <u>Duck Soup.</u> *I was instantly captivated by the intensity, the spontaneity, the playfulness, the daring of improv. The best of childhood all over again!*

Performing improv comedy is a joy. And it's a joy to introduce improv to teens, younger adults, and older adults whose initial terror is often right there on their faces when they enter the room for their first session. It's deeply satisfying to see students break through that terror, become more relaxed, and eventually let loose beautifully.

Years ago, when I first told an L.A. friend about my improv teaching, she was incredulous: "Bob Lamm is teaching improv???" Often I feel that way myself, especially when I remember who I was in 1966. It still shocks me.

42 The Best Thing to Say

In the late 1990s, I'd quit writing sociology textbooks and was looking to do some volunteer work. I went to a teen center in lower Manhattan, The Door, where many of the young people are African American or Latinx and are from low-income neighborhoods. When a staff member mentioned their outstanding art program, I inquired about theater and was shocked to learn that they had no such program. I mentioned I'd taken a lot of improv classes and perhaps I could offer something.

My thought was perhaps to run improv comedy sessions, but things took an unexpected turn. I met staff members from the education department and began using improv to help run practice job interviews for an employment skills class. Then I went into English as a Second Language (ESL) classes and ran improv exercises with recent immigrants from China. Eventually some members of the counseling staff asked if we could work together. In the end, I was a volunteer at The Door for two years and ran 66 workshops, some comedy but many using role-playing to build skills or to examine sensitive issues.

A counselor named Seth asked me about working with one of his groups. It had five young guys, mainly Latinx. The group's focus was making connections with other people; Seth said that was a problem for many teenagers. I'd never done anything like this and had had no relevant training.

But I was eager to give it a try and I'd have a counselor there with me.

I explained that we would do the same exercise various times. Two friends would meet. Friend A would have a serious emotional problem that he didn't want to talk about. Friend B would try to get Friend A to open up. A could decide what to do. If he initially didn't open up, B would keep trying other approaches. Right through to the end, it would be A's choice to open up or keep his secret.

One teen, Mike, immediately insisted that he didn't want to be in a scene. Over two decades of teaching improv, I've never forced anyone to be part of a scene. I told him it was fine to just sit and watch. We did the exercise twice with different participants. The scenes went fairly well. Suddenly Mike said quite emphatically: "I want to be in a scene!" I said that was great. I set up a new scene with Mike as Friend B and Antonio as Friend A.

Antonio began the scene loudly and decisively: "OK, I've got a problem, and I don't want to talk about it!" Mike stayed calm. He quietly said, "Hey, that's fine. You definitely don't have to talk about it if you don't want to. But maybe it would help to talk about it." Antonio was insistent. He wasn't going to talk about what was wrong. Absolutely not.

Mike held to his task. Very gently and uncritically, he kept encouraging Antonio to open up. Finally, Antonio almost exploded: "Why should I tell you? You wouldn't understand anyway!" Mike wasn't shaken. He said softly: "You know, you're right. I might not understand. All I can say is 'I'll try to understand.'"

This was the single best moment of my two decades of teaching improv. I was profoundly moved. We've all had times where we've shared something painful and someone rushed into saying "I understand" when they obviously didn't. What better thing can anyone say in life than "I'll try to understand"?

43 <u>Our Men in Uniform</u>

I live at 172 West 79th Street, corner of Amsterdam Avenue, in Manhattan's Upper West Side. My father's two sisters, Frieda and Amy Lamm, moved into apartment #6E sometime in the late 1930s. My parents married in 1943 and moved into #6F. I was born in 1947 and eventually we moved into #2G, a bigger apartment. We moved to the suburbs in 1955; my aunts remained in #6E. Amy died in the 1960s. In 1971, Frieda had to go into a nursing home and I moved into my aunts' apartment. I've been here ever since. Someone from my family has lived in this apartment for more than 80 years!

As a boy, I could see that my parents and aunts always had a warm relationship with the guys who worked in the building. My childhood favorite, elevator operator George Banks, had become the superintendent by the time I began living at 172 in my early 20s. George and his wife Sadie were ministers at a small church in Harlem. My family had always had a special connection to them. In Frieda's last months living in #6E, she began to deteriorate cognitively. She'd wake up, see on her clock that it was 4:00, and decide to go out shopping. Only it might be 4:00 in the morning. The night elevator man couldn't stop her. He'd wake up George, who'd go out on the street and search till he found Frieda.

In my 20s, quite a few of the building workers were George's relatives. I played basketball with these African

American men in a nearby schoolyard. I went to one of their homes in Queens for a family barbecue. When the landlord tried to evict me, they stood with me and, despite pressure, wouldn't lie in court. They told me stories about the racism they faced from tenants and I began to see it myself. Some tenants treated these guys, working in service jobs, as "servants" in a classic, ugly way.

Over time, even as the staff changed (and became increasingly Latinx), I built strong connections with these men and spoke out on their behalf. It seemed a family tradition and now it was my turn to keep it going. Then in 2006, I began the 172 Interview Project. I interviewed those building employees who consented, wrote profiles of each averaging more than 1000 words, and distributed the profiles to all residents. My hope was that through this project residents would better appreciate the men who helped them every day.

In 2006 and early 2007, I distributed five profiles, all well received. I didn't have publication in mind. But two friends outside the building, both involved in oral history, pushed me. In the end, the *New York Times* published a full-page color photo essay, "Our Men in Uniform," for which I wrote the text. The piece drew on the profiles and included direct quotes from each man. They were thrilled, I was thrilled, residents of the building were thrilled. And, most wonderfully, these guys—many living in neighborhoods where the *New York Times* was hardly everywhere—were being recognized on the street!

One of those five, our handyman Jose Santiago, had become a dear friend. I spent time with him and his family off the job, including six of us having a huge all-you-can-eat Chinese lunch in Flushing, Queens. In his profile, Jose recalled how difficult it was for him as a teenager when his family moved from a heavily Puerto Rican neighborhood in the Bronx to western Harlem, where there were few Puerto Ricans. His new high school was 90 percent Black and most of the Latinx students were Cuban. "But once I made one friend, it was so easy to make a second friend, and then a third and a fourth," Jose told me during our interview.

In the mid-1980s, Jose was in a bowling league in the Bronx at an alley located right next to Yankee Stadium. He spoke of meeting his wife Tania when she was waitressing there. He wanted some soda and asked for it in a Cuban accent, not knowing that Tania was Cuban. It was love at first sight for Jose. He kept talking to her in that accent and she wouldn't say anything. Eventually, when she found out that Jose wasn't Cuban, she called her mother and said: "Ma, I just met this Puerto Rican who says he's Cuban! I'm mixed up!"

Tragically, in 2008, a year after his photo appeared in the *New York Times,* Jose had a massive stroke. He never regained consciousness and died within a day or two. I visited the hospital and saw Jose, but he never saw me. I was honored to be one of the speakers at his wake. I'll always miss him.

44 <u>Race and Class at a Posh Hotel</u>

In 2009, I spent three wonderful weeks in New Zealand. On my way home, at the beginning of a two-day stopover in Los Angeles, I took a shuttle van from the airport to the Georgian Hotel, the 80-year-old Art Deco hotel in Santa Monica where I'd stayed many times. I immediately liked my van driver, so I sat in the passenger seat to chat with him. On first glance, I guessed he was African American, but actually he was from western Africa.

We stopped outside a high-priced hotel in Santa Monica to let another passenger out. I knew I'd soon be at the Georgian, but we couldn't leave. The loop toward the hotel's exit was blocked—only because the driver of the unmarked van in front of us had his door completely open as he spoke with one of the parking attendants.

We waited. I was tired. I'm a New Yorker; I rarely sit there quietly while something annoying is happening. I asked the van driver to encourage them to get out of our way. There was no need to move the front van, just move their conversation a few feet. My driver asked in a nice, reasonable way but they didn't move. I was not happy.

Then the parking attendant brought in a manager—a South Asian man wearing a sport jacket with an insignia—to speak with the driver of the front van. We were still blocked. Again, I asked my driver to intervene. Again, he asked them quite nicely to move. The manager flatly refused. He said he wouldn't move, that we would have to wait, that this was the hotel's property. Now I was furious.

We continued to wait. Finally the conversation ended and the driver of the front van closed his door. We began a slow exit. The manager stood there, quite near us. With my window open, I angrily shouted: "How about some courtesy?" To my astonishment, he began apologizing profusely.

That really set me off. "How can you do that?" I yelled. "You're sorry about treating *me* that way because I'm white, but it's fine to treat *him* (my van driver) the exact same way because he's Black!" We drove off. The driver and I shared our disgust at what we'd just witnessed.

The next morning I returned to that hotel and registered a protest with a young white manager (who said he was "shocked"), an impressive African American security officer (who did not seem shocked), and the hotel's head of security. I told each of them that this type of racism is unacceptable no matter which groups are involved in what way.

I had a bad feeling right away about the head of security, an older white man. Sure enough, he offered a variety of dodges—most notably that the hotel contracts the work in the parking area to an outside firm. Therefore neither the parking guy nor his manager were employees of the hotel. I countered: "Their work is conducted on hotel property and obviously it reflects on your hotel."

My initial reaction to this incident was to focus on the lack of courtesy (it would have taken so little effort to let our van leave) and the blatant racism. But, on reflection, class was a major factor as well. It's possible that a parking manager for a posh hotel would have reacted in the same way if he, the van driver, and I were all white… or were all South Asian… or were all Black (whether African or African American). All we can be sure of in this instance was that the lack of courtesy toward a van driver with Black skin was considered appropriate and defensible, whereas the exact same lack of courtesy toward a van passenger with white skin was deemed grounds for a strong apology.

The murders of Eric Garner, Breonna Taylor, George Floyd, and others have been a vivid reminder that we still have a long way to go in addressing racism, classism, sexism and other forms of bigotry and discrimination. But sometimes it's the "little things," like what happened in that hotel entrance and afterward, that are hard to get past because they're endless.

45 The Bronx Underbelly Tour

In spring 2009, I read in the *New York Times* that Curtis Sliwa and the Guardian Angels (best known for their safety patrols of communities) were leading free "Bronx Underbelly" tours. These walks took people around the South Bronx to show ways in which that neighborhood had changed for the better since the violence of the 1970s—and ways in which the area hadn't changed much. The tours immediately became controversial because the Borough President of the Bronx, Adolfo Carrion, Jr., hated the name, claiming it hurt the image of the borough by dredging up the worst memories of the past.

I'm always eager to explore New York City and have been doing so in a dedicated way since the late 1990s. I was excited to go on one of these tours. On a sunny spring day, we hopped on a Manhattan subway and headed to the South Bronx. Curtis Sliwa, a few Guardian Angels in uniform, and about a dozen of us. Some from New York City, some foreign tourists. All that we saw and learned was fascinating, but three parts stood out:

One Sliwa began by taking us to a school playground where kids were happily engaged in routine games and activities. He pointed to a spot where some of the pavement was red. Sliwa said that in the first year of the Guardian Angels one of their members had died right there.

On a weekend day, a boy on the autism spectrum had disappeared, presumably wandering somewhere in the community. There was no suspicion of foul play. People all over the neighborhood were looking for him, including the Guardian Angels. In the 1970s, this playground had been controlled by a street gang. On weekends, the gang often brought in bands to play there. It was thought that perhaps the kid might have heard music and wandered over.

Two Guardian Angels went to the playground to look around, carrying a photo of the missing boy. They approached some gang members, made it clear they wanted no trouble, told them of the autistic kid, and asked the gang members if they'd seen him. Without any warning, one of the gang guys pulled out a gun and shot one of the Guardian Angels in the stomach. He fell to the ground. The shooter pointed his gun at the fallen Angel, ready to ensure he'd complete the killing. But the second Guardian Angel jumped on top of the first to protect him. The gang member shot a second time. The Guardian Angel protecting his friend died. The guy who'd initially been shot eventually survived.

Apparently they'd painted over where the blood was. Sliwa told us that the playground was no longer controlled by any gang. One example of improvements in the South Bronx.

Two Sliwa took us to a street corner about two blocks from the original Yankee Stadium (still in use at that time). We could see it from the corner. Diagonally across from us was a bodega with a few young guys standing outside, seemingly doing nothing. In fact, these guys were waiting to engage in drug deals.

At that same intersection, Sliwa pointed to the building in front of us with a large mural on a wall facing the street. He explained that the mural had been created to honor a deceased drug dealer. For years, parents and neighbors had pushed to get that mural removed. They didn't want young kids to see artwork glorifying a dealer. They went to the local police and were told that the NYPD couldn't do anything because the mural was on private property. Only the building's owner could remove the mural. Then the parents and neighbors met with the owner. He wouldn't take action, obviously frightened of possible retaliation from the drug dealers. So the mural remained on that wall. One example of how the same old problems of the South Bronx were still there.

Three Here's a question I've asked many people since I went on the Bronx Underbelly Tour. I'd never have gotten it right; almost no one I've asked has. Suppose you're walking on a city street. You see above you electrical lines, perhaps 12 feet high, extending across the street. On top of those lines you see pairs of sneakers or running shoes, laced together and thrown over the electrical wires. Why? What does this mean?

Sliwa took us to a side street in the South Bronx. There were sneakers and running shoes over the wires high above us. He asked for our guesses as to why this had been done. I thought perhaps older kids were bullying younger kids, taking their sneakers, and throwing them over the electrical lines. I was so wrong!!!

Suppose you have money, live in a wealthy suburb like Scarsdale, and want to buy some cocaine, crack, or heroin. You don't want to do this anywhere near your home, where someone you know may see you. So you decide you'll go to the South Bronx to score some drugs. The shoes hanging from the electrical wires send a message: you're in the exact right place, indeed a safe place, to make your purchase.

You stop your car. A young kid runs out. He tells you exactly where to go in the adjoining building. He'll watch your car. You go to the designated apartment or window, pay them, get your drugs, and leave. No one will mess with you. The dealers want this street to be safe for the rich guys. They will *not* allow other criminals to attack clients and threaten their drug trade. So that's why all those sneakers are up there!

I'm not an admirer of Curtis Sliwa's politics. But I will always have a great debt to him and the Guardian Angels for that profoundly educational afternoon.

46 A Jewish Boy Goes to Poland

I never thought I'd go to Poland, where so many Jews died in Auschwitz, Treblinka, Sobibor, the Warsaw Ghetto, and elsewhere. But unexpectedly I made a Polish friend in London, then another, and found myself with an invitation. So in 2009 I spent eight days in Warsaw, Auschwitz, Birkenau, and Krakow.

Warsaw

Just thinking about Warsaw has always given me chills because of my intense feelings about the Warsaw Ghetto revolt, the high point of Jewish resistance to the Nazis. In his book *Uprising in the Warsaw Ghetto,* Ber Mark describes this revolt as "an unparalleled example of bravery in the face of imminent destruction."

Since my 20s, I've remembered the fighters of the Warsaw Ghetto by reading a passage from that book at Passover seders. The revolt began on April 19, 1943. That very night, at 5 Karmelicka (Street) in Warsaw, traditional Jews celebrated the first night of the Passover holiday. In the words of an eyewitness, Ghetto fighter Simkha Korngold:

> Five men stand watch outside with weapons in hand. My father sits in the bunker conducting the Seder. Two candles illuminate the cups of wine.

> To us, it appears the cups are filled with blood. All of us who sit here are the sacrifice. When "pour out your wrath" is recited we all shudder. We've awaited a miracle, but none appears. (From Ber Mark, *Uprising in the Warsaw Ghetto,* Schocken, 1975, p. 29.)

Those words always held deep meaning for me. But now a Polish friend and I were walking on the very streets where the Warsaw Ghetto revolt was launched, where courageous battles were fought against impossible odds. We saw markings on the ground where the ghetto walls had been. We saw memorials to the Uprising and to the ghetto fighters.

Most important for me, we went to Karmelicka. There is no longer a number 5 on that street; a small grocery store stands on the ground where the Seder in 1943 probably took place. But I stood on that spot.

Auschwitz

With Polish friends, I stood before the infamous entrance gate which still declares—with unspeakably bitter irony—"Arbeit Macht Frei" (Work Makes You Free).

Having been at the U.S. Holocaust Memorial Museum in Washington, D.C., and the Yad Vashem in Jerusalem, the many horrific photos at Auschwitz of Jewish prisoners alive and dead, and of survivors at the time of liberation, were not new to me. What haunted me most at Auschwitz were the shoes. Suddenly before us were small shoes, taken from children soon to die. So many. Then a much larger pile of adult-sized shoes, a pile that seemed to go on and on. I will never forget those shoes.

Birkenau

After Auschwitz, we drove two miles down the road to Birkenau, the much larger of the two nearby death camps. As we walked around, I saw two dozen Israeli teenagers with their guides. One young woman was wearing a yellow Jewish star along with a number. Attached to her shirt, her sign said (in English): "This is the number of my Zaida" (her grandfather).

I began speaking with her and her friend, but I was overcome and almost incoherent. I pointed to her sign. I cried. They seemed to understand. A little later, she told me that her Romanian grandfather had been in Auschwitz, had been moved to a work camp, had survived, was still alive, and had seven grandchildren.

Krakow

I stayed in Kazimierz, the former Jewish ghetto of Krakow, and saw the Jewish sights. On my last morning there, I spoke with a non-Jewish Pole serving breakfast at my hotel. A university student, she was following the path of both her parents by studying law. But against their wishes, she was also studying the Jewish culture of Poland. Her particular interests were Hasidism and the history of Galician Jews. She told me she hoped to visit Israel. She was unfamiliar with the novels of Chaim Potok, so I encouraged her to read *The Chosen* and *My Name Is Asher Lev.*

As I headed for the Warsaw/Chopin airport and my flights home, I wondered: wouldn't it have been wonderful if somehow I could have brought together the impressive Israeli teenager with her yellow star and the equally impressive young Polish woman eager to learn about Jewish culture?

47 <u>A Master Teacher at Work</u>

In 2010, I was in Edinburgh and visited the Scottish Museum of Art, right in the center of the city. I strolled into a room not realizing that it had been set aside for a special exhibition on artists' views of dance and dancers. All around the room were paintings and sculptures of dancers, some by Degas. (Who, by the way, was a rabid anti-Semite.)

I was stunned to see a young woman in a ballerina costume in the middle of the room. She actually *was* a ballerina but was there that day as a model. Adults with easels were drawing or painting her. She was posing for about 10 minutes at a time. A man who seemed to be in charge was running around the room talking to people at easels.

It looked like an art class, but it wasn't, at least in the sense I initially assumed. The museum had brought in a local artist and art teacher, Darren, to run the exhibition. The artists weren't his students from an ongoing class; they were simply museum visitors who'd wandered into the room. Darren had persuaded them to sit down at easels and start drawing or painting the model. When I realized this, I was overwhelmed. It's intimidating enough for most of us who never draw or paint to consider doing so in private. But publicly, with a model? In a setting where anyone passing by can watch us and look (perhaps quite critically) at our efforts?

For about five minutes, I observed as Darren zoomed around the room. I realized he was a genius, a master teacher. More than anything, he was dealing with fear, just as I do in teaching improv to beginners and nonperformers. He was instantly getting total strangers to do something that many probably found rather scary. Why was he successful? He had such a love of art, such passion, such enthusiasm, that it was infectious. As the finest teachers do, whatever the subject. When I'd taught high school decades earlier, there was a chemistry teacher just like that. His absolute love for science was impossible to resist. The same with Darren and art.

I spoke briefly with this extraordinary teacher, sung his praises, and headed on my way to see the rest of the museum. But soon I returned to watch him some more. Only then did I notice that as he quickly moved from student to student he was actually criticizing their work. I saw him tell one woman that the upper parts of her painting were great but she needed to work a bit more on the ballerina's legs. He quickly explained why and how. She took it all in, with no apparent resistance. With a different instructor, these students might have argued or bolted. But Darren was so gentle, so captivating, so encouraging, that they accepted both his praise and his constructive criticism.

Imagine what our world would be like if we had *lots* of teachers—in all subjects, for students at all age levels—like Darren.

48 <u>The Understudy</u>

As someone who loves theater, I've seen many superb actors, many remarkable plays, but also two priceless moments that happened *immediately after* the performances ended. One involved a star, the other didn't.

• •

In 1996, while in London, I saw a revival of Lionel Bart's musical *Oliver,* brilliantly adapted from the Charles Dickens novel *Oliver Twist.* My parents had seen the original London production decades earlier and had become devoted fans of Lionel Bart's work. Now, finally, I was seeing one of his musicals.

Jim Dale was starring as the evil Fagin. *Oliver* requires lots of child actors, a few in crucial roles. The matinee performance I saw was magnificent, with great work from Dale and the child leads. When it ended, the audience erupted in a joyous standing ovation. Then Dale silenced the crowd. He explained that under relevant British laws—more stringent than in the U.S.—the child actors could only perform on the West End for a certain number of months. We'd just seen their final performance. He recognized them and thanked them with one of the most moving public statements I've ever seen. I've always viewed Jim Dale as a hero for his beautiful remarks that day. Surely those child actors and their family members in the audience will cherish that day forever.

• •

In 2014, I went to the Manhattan Theatre Club's production of a new play by Sarah Treem, *When We Were Young and Unafraid.* It's set in the early 1970s and is about a middle-aged woman living in a rural area who hides in her home women who've been badly beaten by their husbands.

I went because I'd known women at that time who were among the earliest activists in assisting such abused women. I'd known a woman who had done in real life exactly what the central character of the play had done. I went because Cherry Jones and Zoe Kazan had the lead roles. And I went because young Morgan Saylor was playing Jones's teenage daughter. I'd loved her work in the early seasons of the Showtime series *Homeland* as Nicholas Brody's daughter Dana.

As the first act continued, I realized the play, with its admirable intentions, just wasn't working for me. It was addressing many—alas, too many--issues about feminism, male violence against women, love, and adolescence. It was completely well-intentioned, but despite fine performances I found *When We Were Young and Unafraid* muddled and unsatisfying.

Intermission went on longer than usual. Finally someone came onstage and explained that there would be a further delay. An understudy, Caitlin McGee, would replace Zoe Kazan for the remainder of the performance. I later heard that Kazan had sprained her ankle. Her character had to climb up and down a ladder to the house's unseen attic and that must have been what led to the injury.

Caitlin McGee did extremely well under these difficult circumstances. In decades as a theatergoer, I'd never seen an understudy take over midway, though I know it happens. Moreover, as I was later told, McGee had never done a performance of the show before. Suddenly she was thrown out there after intermission!

When the play ended, the cast (apart from Kazan) was onstage and everyone was enthusiastically applauding. The audience seemed to appreciate the play more than I had. The actors were in a line, with Cherry Jones in the center, Morgan Saylor on the extreme left, and Caitlin McGee next to Saylor. They took bows as a group. No stepping forward for individual applause.

It seemed time for the curtain call to end, but suddenly came a surprising moment. Morgan Saylor stepped away from the line, pointed at Caitlin McGee, and encouraged the audience to give McGee a special moment of applause. The audience responded quite warmly and McGee certainly looked delighted. Cherry Jones or any of the older cast members could have done that, but they didn't. Morgan Saylor, only 20 years old at the time, saw what needed to be done and made it happen.

I hung around after the show. Only two other audience members were waiting and one was obviously hoping to get Cherry Jones to sign his program. Eventually I was able to tell Caitlin McGee what a courageous and convincing job she'd done under such difficult circumstances. She seemed thrilled that an audience member had stayed to congratulate her. A few understudies, surely waiting to take out McGee to celebrate, saw what I was doing and seemed quite happy for her.

Then Morgan Saylor appeared. I told her I'd loved her work in *Homeland* and in the play. But, most important, I told her that she should be really proud of what she'd just done for her young colleague.

Little things matter. They did that night.

49 The Train Ride Across Canada

I've done three thrilling train rides. The first was on Scotland's West Highlands Line, which goes from Glasgow through Fort William to Mallaig, a small, lovely fishing village on the country's west coast. This journey includes seeing and going over the Glenfinnan Viaduct, now famous thanks to all the Harry Potter films. The second was on New Zealand's TranzAlpine, which crosses that nation's south island, running between Greymouth and Christchurch.

In 2015, I finally took a train ride I'd had in mind since the early 1970s. After a few days in Toronto, I took The Canadian all the way to Vancouver. Four nights, three days. Absolutely wonderful but for one unexpected problem.

I'd shelled out for a nice little room with a private sink and toilet. I shared a shower at the end of the train car. My room had a combined couch (for daytime) and bed (for nighttime) which stewards would open and close. There was a nice view from my window, but far better were a couple of train cars that were all glass at the top and sides. Because I'd paid enough to have a room, I had three free meals per day in the dining car. The food was excellent. Not excellent for train food, but excellent for anywhere.

We left Toronto midevening. Our first full day consisted almost entirely of passing by lakes and rivers. Endlessly beautiful. The next day we proceeded mainly through rural areas and farmland. Some of it dull to the eye, some of it quite remarkable. On the morning of our last full day, we approached and entered Jasper. To our right, the Canadian Rockies, with their snowy tops, were riveting. Our final morning took us along a river, then we pulled into Vancouver.

The dining car proved to be a continuing problem and it had nothing to do with the superb food and service. All tables were for four and I was on my own. I was seated with an assortment of passengers throughout the trip. Everyone at my tables was pleasant enough and some were quite interesting. But hearing the conversations at adjoining tables didn't help my digestion.

Who can afford that journey for four nights and three days with a comfortable room? Some passengers couldn't, slept in regular seats, and brought their own food. Some purchased an occasional meal in the dining car. But mainly that car was filled with affluent white Canadians, middle-aged and older; affluent whites from the U.S., middle-aged and older; a group of affluent white Australian tourists, middle-aged and older; and a few people of Asian descent. I overheard many conversations that were seriously anti-immigrant, racist, and Islamophobic. I decided not to confront what was being said. This was a vacation; I wasn't looking for political skirmishes.

But when something came right at me… that was different.

For the first night and the first full day, the steward for our car was Ibrahim, a Black man from Senegal in his mid-20s. We hit it off immediately when he learned I was a writer. Ibrahim had been in Canada for two years, was now both working on the train crew and studying at a university, and hoped himself to become a writer. I gave him a few of my articles and he loved them. We had terrific conversations. Alas, early on our second full day, we reached Winnipeg and a completely new train crew took over. I gave Ibrahim my business card and he promised to contact me, but never did. I hope he is still writing and having success.

The steward for the last two days of our journey was Bill, a middle-aged white Canadian. He seemed quite nice and all was fine until the train made a brief stop. This happened periodically along the route and was always a welcome opportunity for passengers and crew to step outside, get some fresh air, and walk around a bit.

At the side of the train, I got into a conversation with Bill, just the two of us. Suddenly he began ranting about how terrible Asians were. I was stunned and livid. I made an instant decision. Bill would be helping me for two more days, including entering my room to close and then reopen the bed. Confronting his racism right then could make those encounters and others rather unpleasant. I resolved that I would say nothing till we were nearing Vancouver. But then I surely would.

Things remained pleasant with Bill over those days. An hour before we reached Vancouver, I found him in the passageway and asked him to be sure to come to my room before we pulled into the train station. When he came, I said I had two things to tell him. I thanked him warmly for the excellent job he'd done and gave him a very good tip (just as I had to Ibrahim). Bill was grateful. Then I told him I detested what he'd said to me about Asians, that it was racist, and how dare he assume it would be OK to say that to me just because I'm white! He looked quite shocked, especially right on the heels of my kind words and good tip.

Bill began "I want to explain...." Over decades, I've almost always found that when someone wants to "explain" their bigoted remarks the explanation is generally worse than the initial remarks. I feared what was next. But, remarkably, Bill stopped himself. He paused—and then did a complete turnaround. He said that his remarks had been wrong, that he shouldn't have said them, that he was really sorry. He seemed genuinely sincere. I was shocked. I thanked him for his apology, we shook hands, and said a warm goodbye.

It was, on the whole, a memorable journey I'd surely recommend to anyone who loves scenic train rides. But, in an important way, that surprising conversation with Bill was the highlight.

50 <u>The Imposter</u>

The imposter is me. Well, maybe.

I've had a strange life in many ways, certainly including my careers as a writer and a teacher. My highest degree is a B.A. Never went to law school, never went to graduate school. I have somehow managed, especially in terms of teaching, to get lots of jobs for which I didn't have the standard qualifications. I've never lied on a resume or in an interview. I've never pretended to be anything I'm not. But somehow I've apparently been good in talking my way into some exciting, challenging opportunities for which I was arguably unqualified.

I've taught preschool, 9th and 10th grade English, 11th and 12th grade history, for-credit college classes with students in their teens and early 20s, noncredit Continuing Ed. literature classes mainly with older students, and improv with adults of all ages and teenagers. I've taught students ages 3 to 85 and just about every age in between—and have loved just about all of it.

• •

The first major issue about being an imposter came when I fell into teaching improv comedy for beginners and non-performers. I've been successful: many, many students have loved my work. I tell everyone that 90% of what I do in improv comedy classes and workshops isn't really teaching. Instead, it's doing everything I can to create a warm, safe, supportive, encouraging atmosphere where students can relax and let loose. When that happens, the class is almost certain to be a big hit. (*The five principles I've developed for my improv teaching are in Appendix A.*)

At times, though, I struggle with feeling like an imposter. Often that happens when students discover that I'm not a performer and I see the expressions on their faces. Also when I'm reminded that there are so many improv teachers out there whose knowledge and experience is miles beyond mine.

Before I began teaching improv, I took ongoing classes or one-time workshops with at least a dozen improv teachers. The very best was Karl; I worked with him for a few years. His understanding of improv was brilliant. The challenges he posed for students in warmups and scenes were varied and stimulating. His comments and critiques were incisive. Alas, he sometimes treated students like crap. I felt that too often and eventually I left.

Years later, when I was teaching "The Joy of Improv" at the City University of New York Graduate Center, I had a new student named Wally who loved our class. One day we discovered that we'd both taken Karl's classes in different time periods. We agreed that Karl was a knowledgeable and talented teacher, but ultimately admitted that we'd both left in disgust. Wally shared lavish praise for my work. Did that make me conclude that I'm a better improv teacher than Karl? No way. But it did help me to feel less like an imposter.

• •

In 2007, after a decade of teaching improv, I loved and was committed to that work but wanted to add something new to my teaching. Something more political. So I began teaching noncredit college literature classes. As of 2021, I've taught "Novels With a Social Conscience 15 times (using 36 different novels); "Plays With a Social Conscience" seven times (using 28 plays); and "Memoirs With a Social Conscience" three times (using 18 memoirs or works of personal nonfiction). Most of these Continuing Education classes have been at New York University's School of Professional Studies. *(The list of readings I've assigned is in Appendix B.)*

My classes are run mainly like seminars. I begin with a 10 to 15 minute lecture about the writer whose work we've just read. But class discussion, in which I pose questions and am active, is crucial. For some of my students, fortunately a small proportion, that approach is unacceptable. They want a traditional classroom: the instructor speaks, they listen, and perhaps ask an occasional question. They come to learn from the teacher; it's a one-way process. By contrast, at the first session of every literature course, I tell my students that my views are just that: my views. Not the authoritative statement on any author or work of literature. I underscore that reactions to literature or any art form are very personal. I encourage students to state their reactions and opinions and to challenge me or each other when it feels right. I argue that the best type of literature classroom is one where we all learn from each other.

My classes have gone quite well. I've received two glowing observation reports from administrators--as well as many wonderful, grateful responses from students in person, in e-mails, and in anonymous student evaluations. (Of course I've occasionally been scorched!) Nevertheless, I know there are instructors in my program and everywhere else with far greater understanding of literature, literary history, literary analysis, and critical approaches to the study of literature. So I struggle with feeling like an imposter.

In spring 2019, it came to a head. It was the first session of a new NYU class on "Memoirs With a Social Conscience." That afternoon we'd be discussing the first of Frederick Douglass's three superb memoirs, *Narrative of the Life of Frederick Douglass, An American Slave.* It was a small class, only eight students. Some who'd worked with me before, some new.

I always begin the first session of any course with intro-ductions. As we went around the room, it was the turn of a new student, Roger Cooper. He briefly mentioned that he was 75 years old and a retired publisher. He was completely modest, but as I listened I was certain he had had a very distinguished career in the publishing world. That, among other achievements, he had worked with and become friends with many famous, outstanding authors. Eventually it became clear that I'd been right, though he remained modest.

When Roger finished his introduction, I had a moment of internal panic. This was the moment of truth I'd been fearing for so long! This was the person who would definitively realize that I'm an imposter. Roger was so obviously warm, sensitive, and generous that I wasn't afraid he'd expose me in front of the other students. But he'd *know*.

The class plunged into Frederick Douglass's life and work. Roger and other students, including my terrific friend Kevin Beauchamp, offered insightful comments. When I occasionally glanced at Roger, he seemed interested and engaged. The next week we discussed Art Spiegelman's *Maus*. Again Roger was actively involved and seemed excited by the way the class was proceeding. I was a bit stunned.

Throughout the sessions of that class, Roger's enthusiasm was evident. When it ended, he told me he planned to take my fall class on "Novels With a Social Conscience." He did and I was lucky to make a wonderful new friend. He's had lovely things to say about my literature teaching. And it's surely made me feel less like an imposter.

CONCLUSION

In 1966, in that memorable night alone in a Yale dorm room, I decided I was boring and didn't want to be. I didn't want to fulfill my parents' dreams; I wanted a more authentic life. I knew I'd have to take risks, meet a far more diverse range of people, put myself in new and challenging situations. I feel I've done that. Both at best and at worst, I've had a life that feels authentic and I hope to continue doing so for many more years.

Of course I have regrets. Of course there have been many challenges that I wish I'd handled differently. But I've had lots of fascinating adventures, far more than 50. I've known and continue to know many remarkable people. I've lived as much as possible on my terms. I feel lucky.

One last thought. The only thing in life that I'm evangelical about is writing. I'm always encouraging people to do writing, especially personal writing drawn from their lives. Journals, personal essays, creative nonfiction, plays, short stories, poems, songs, memoirs, novels, whatever. I've shared 50 stories from my life. Everyone has stories worth telling and worth hearing. Write yours!

ACKNOWLEDGMENTS

Roger Cooper has been crucial in the creation and shaping of this book. Without knowing that for many years I'd been pondering writing a memoir, he twice encouraged me to do so. That was the final push I needed. Because of Rog's outstanding career as a publisher, I asked him to serve as a consultant on this project. His insightful recommendations and consistent support have been a very special gift.

Five other friends were kind enough to read and comment on the entire manuscript: Kevin Beauchamp, Ann Olivarius, CindyAnn Rose-Redwood, Reuben Rose-Redwood, and Carrie Treadwell. Each offered important reactions, criticisms, and enthusiasm. I am in their debt. (Ann Olivarius was one of the plaintiffs in *Alexander v. Yale,* the pioneering late 1970s lawsuit on sexual harassment discussed in story #12.)

The following friends read at least a few stories each and contributed helpful perspectives: Steve Brier, Pat Del Rey, Lisa Dennett, Rebecca Elbogen, Aaron Greenberg, Reilly Hilbert, Kevin Hodges, Carlos Horrillo, Carla Horwitz, David Henry Hwang, and Agata Luczynska. They all have my thanks.

Elsa Peterson Obuchowski offered her expertise regarding copyright and permissions issues. George Robinson shared book proposals that were very helpful to read. Tim Sheard offered useful advice regarding publishing options as well as valuable contacts. It was Tim who connected me with the wonderful Dave Bass, who worked with me and skillfully guided me through the process of self-publishing this book. One of the many joys of this book was working with Dave. He even allowed me to make a few stylistic choices that would horrify some of his friends. I take full responsibility!

I've been a proud member of the National Writers Union since it was founded in 1981. It's worth noting that it was through the NWU that I met George and Tim and that Elsa and Dave are NWU members.

I am deeply grateful to everyone named above.

APPENDIX A   Five Principles of Improv

In every improv comedy class or workshop that I run, I share five basic principles with students. In a class that runs for a semester, I restate these principles in every session. I believe that hearing them again and again has great value for introductory students. My friend Elizabeth Lorris Ritter, who took my class over a number of semesters and then began teaching improv herself, has said that these are excellent principles for all of life. She's right.

1. *Commitment, Intensity, Concentration, High Energy Level.* We're doing short scenes. It's essential not to hold back, to completely focus and throw yourself into the work. This doesn't mean being outrageous or explosive in every scene. For example, you might choose to have your character be shy. If so, we don't want you to be sort-of-shy; you should be *very* shy. If you're an astronaut, an opera singer, the ruler of a monarchy, whatever—you've got to totally throw yourself into that character.

2. *Play, Relax, This Isn't a Professional Class.* New improv students often worry that they'll make a mistake in a scene. In improv, mistakes aren't such a big deal. An audience won't even notice many of them. Most important, 20 minutes later almost no one will remember your mistake. But this is essential: you

can *never* stop in an improv scene. You can't ask the teacher a question while the scene is on. You *must* keep going no matter what. It's like being onstage in a very serious Broadway drama when an actor accidentally knocks over a lamp. It crashes to the ground and breaks, making a very loud noise. The actors must keep going. If someone can come up with a great improv line— perhaps "I always hated that lamp!"—you do that. Otherwise you have to ignore the broken lamp and just continue onward.

3. *Teamwork, Make Your Partner Look Good, Be Sure to Listen.* Improv is challenging and teamwork is essential. You must pay attention to every word your partners say, to every gesture or facial expression. You are in this together. The attitude has to be: if the scene works, we all take credit; if the scene doesn't work, we all take responsibility. If your attitude is "I'm doing great in this scene and my partners aren't up to my level," that's deadly. Moreover, if you see that one of your partners is struggling, it's your job to try to help them in any way possible.

4. *Say "Yes," Accept Offers.* Ideas for where to take a scene (sometimes called "offers" by improv teachers) are crucial for success. If a partner introduces an idea, it's essential to say "yes" and go with that. Saying "no" can be a serious problem. Suppose two of us are alone on a deserted island. We have no food, no water, no means of transportation

to get off the island, no means of communication to call for help. We literally have nothing. Suppose your partner says "Let's build a rocket ship and get out of here!" and you respond "That's a stupid idea." Now you're back to nothing, the audience has seen that idea die, and your partner may be shaken by your negative response. It's far better to say an enthusiastic "yes," grab some imaginary rocks, and begin building the rocket ship. This is improv; it doesn't have to be realistic. You can use those rocks to build the rocket ship and then zoom off that island to safety!

5. *No Stereotypes.* The first four principles I share with students are emphasized in one way or another by almost every improv teacher. I learned them all as a student. But this final principle is something none of my many teachers ever said. I encourage my improv students everywhere to avoid all the too-familiar stereotypes of our culture regarding gender, race, ethnicity, nationality, religion, social class, sexual orientation, gender identity, age, disability, and any others that are appropriate. The world of comedy is too often a world of bigotry. Some who love comedy insist that you can't have humor without these persistent stereotypes. It's simply a lie. Over two decades, I've seen my students endlessly create hilarious scenes without that ugliness.

APPENDIX B   <u>82 Literary Works Used in My Classes</u>

<u>Novels</u> (35)

Chinua Achebe, *Things Fall Apart*
Isabel Allende, *Of Love and Shadows*
Dorothy Allison, *Bastard Out of Carolina*
James Baldwin, *Giovanni's Room*
James Baldwin, *If Beale Street Could Talk*
Sandra Cisneros, *The House on Mango Street*
Junot Diaz, *The Brief Wondrous Life of Oscar Wao*
Ralph Ellison, *Invisible Man*
Deanna Fei, *A Thread of Sky*
Athol Fugard, *Tsotsi*
Michael Gold, *Jews Without Money*
Nadine Gordimer, *July's People*
Mark Haddon, *The Curious Incident of the Dog in the Night-Time*
Laila Lalami, *Hope and Other Dangerous Pursuits*
Laila Lalami, *The Moor's Account*
Nella Larsen, *Passing*
Edouard Louis, *The End of Eddy*
Mary McCarthy, *The Group*
Carson McCullers, *The Heart Is a Lonely Hunter*
Louise Meriwether, *Daddy Was a Number Runner*
Gloria Naylor, *The Women of Brewster Place*
Celeste Ng, *Everything I Never Told You*
Frank Norris, *The Octopus*
George Orwell, *Animal Farm*
George Orwell, *1984*

Julie Otsuka, *When the Emperor Was Divine*
Philip Roth, *The Plot Against America*
Budd Schulberg, *What Makes Sammy Run?*
Zadie Smith, *White Teeth*
John Steinbeck, *Of Mice and Men*
John Steinbeck, *The Pearl*
Amy Tan, *The Joy Luck Club*
Alice Walker, *The Color Purple*
Robert Penn Warren, *All the King's Men*
Richard Wright, *Native Son*
Anzia Yezierska, *Bread Givers*

Plays (28)

Caryl Churchill, *Cloud Nine*
Caryl Churchill, *Top Girls*
Athol Fugard, *Blood Knot*
Athol Fugard, *Master Harold and the Boys*
Athol Fugard, *My Children, My Africa*
Charles Fuller, *A Soldier's Play*
Lorraine Hansberry, *A Raisin in the Sun*
David Henry Hwang, *M Butterfly*
David Henry Hwang, *Yellow Face*
Henrik Ibsen, *A Doll's House*
Larry Kramer, *The Normal Heart*
Carson McCullers, *The Member of the Wedding*
Arthur Miller, *All My Sons*
Arthur Miller, *The Crucible*
Arthur Miller, *A View from the Bridge*
Dominique Morisseau, *Skeleton Crew*

Lynn Nottage, *Intimate Apparel*
Lynn Nottage, *Ruined*
Clifford Odets, *Awake and Sing*
Nina Raine, *Tribes*
Lisa Ramirez, *Exit Cuckoo*
David Robson, *Man Measures Man*
George Bernard Shaw, *Pygmalion*
Martin Sherman, *Bent*
Anna Deavere Smith, *Fires in the Mirror*
Diana Son, *Stop Kiss*
August Wilson, *Jitney*
August Wilson, *Joe Turner's Come and Gone*

Memoirs and Personal Nonfiction (18)

James Baldwin, *The Fire Next Time*
Alison Bechdel, *Fun/Home: A Family Tragicomedy*
Frederick Douglass, *Narrative of the Life of Frederick Douglass, An American Slave*
Deanna Fei, *Girl in Glass*
Diane Guerrero with Michelle Burford, *In the Country We Love*
Dave Eggers, *Zeitoun*
Barbara Ehrenreich, *Nickel and Dimed*
John Hersey, *Hiroshima*
Jeanne Wakatsuki Houston and James D. Houston, *Farewell to Manzanar*
Harriet Jacobs, *Incidents in the Life of a Slave Girl*
Piper Kerman, *Orange Is the New Black*
Courtney E. Martin and J. Courtney Sullivan (eds.), *Click: When We Knew We Were Feminists*

James McBride, *The Color of Water*
Trevor Noah, *Born a Crime: Stories from a South African Childhood*
Marjane Satrapi, *Persepolis*
Art Spiegelman, *Maus: A Survivor's Tale*
Art Spiegelman, *Maus* II: *And Here My Troubles Began*
Elie Wiesel, *Night*

SOURCES

"Asian Americans and Jewish Americans" (story #7) is adapted from "Christian God and Jewish Man at Yale." Originally published in *Response*, fall 1974, then reprinted in *Jewish Digest,* April 1975.

"The Goldfish Bowl" (#11) is adapted from a piece with the same title published in *Sarah Lawrence*, spring 2010.

"Student Power in the Classroom" (#22), "The Women Students Leave" (#23), and "Sexism in a Sports Class" (#24) are adapted from various versions of "Learning from Women." First published in *Morning Due: A Journal of Men Against Sexism,* Vol. 2, no. 2, 1976. Then in Jon Snodgrass (ed), *For Men Against Sexism: A Book of Readings* (Times Change Press, 1977); in Peter Murphy (ed.), *Feminism and Masculinities* (Oxford University Press, 2004); and in Shira Tarrant (ed.), *Men Speak Out: Views on Gender, Sex, and Power* (Routledge, 2008). Copyright © Bob Lamm 2003.

"Saying Goodbye" (#28) was published in the *New York Times,* August 13, 2000. Copyright © Bob Lamm 2000.

"Liberating Mary" (#30) was published in *Ms. Magazine,* fall 2004. Copyright © Bob Lamm 2003.

"More Time for Healing" (#32) was published in *Solidarity,* March 1996. Copyright © Bob Lamm 1996.

"Our Men in Uniform" (#43) draws on material with the same title published in the *New York Times,* April 15, 2007. Copyright © Bob Lamm 2007.

Made in the USA
Middletown, DE
13 June 2021

42112914R00120